There's not a flat patch of land anywhere to be found. Every field one encounters climbs up then down into the laps of these hills and slopes; and it is only on account of the untiring vigilance of the stone walls that the fields themselves don't spirit away with the enveloping mists scudding through these districts daily.
[*Preface*, The Faraway Paradise]

If agriculture dies,... it will be the death of talent, the death of excellence, the death of every rural art. The sweet sounds that fill even the smallest villages with harmony will fade away. Those noises and activities interwoven into the pattern of a Welshman's life – that actually collude in supporting and maintaining Welsh Society – all of them will be dead and gone.
[1 June 1841]

A Prosperous Welshman ... wears his own wool and brews his own beer; [his] kitchen serves Welsh mutton and [his] wife and daughters wear Welsh clothes that they make for themselves.
[13 November 1841]

The lightning stabs; the thunder peals. Tongues of fire; torrents of cloudburst – the wonderful splendor of the heavens "declaring the glory of God..."
[17 December 1841]

A blue firmament, a laughing sun, warmth; ribbons of stone sparkling through the white snow on the mountainsides; sunny skies. And it's all filled with the sound of birds, dressed in flashing colors, chanting the spirit of joy...all the day long. I sit outside for what seems like ages and let the weight of all this beauty descend upon me and sink into me, and I listen to the voice of creation in all its unflustered calm.
[29 February 1940]

I rise from my seat and gaze, wide-eyed, to my right, to my left, backwards and forwards as magnificent Creation marches past in a steady stream of wonders that appear and disappear one after the other.
[10 May 1940]

I am absolutely flourishing ... amidst such unremitting greenness, accompanied by the constant song of the cuckoos and birds of the fens; by the murmer of streams and brooks; the subtle sounds of cattle grazing and harrows disking; the ewes and lambs bleating absent-mindedly into the void. And everywhere, the small, frail, newly germinated ferns are unfurling their fiddleheads in the warmth of the sun.
[10 May 1940]

No one else is praying for Wales! They're all praying "for our country" instead; and God knows that Wales isn't meant to be included in that expression.
[23 June 1940]

We – you and I – who take this oath in the name of every generation that has preceded us, are honor-bound to deliver our culture intact into the future.
[6 July 1940]

I walk through cloudbursts; I ramble; I run. I soak up the sounds of the rushing waters and the bleating sheep; I'm almost completely at one with the peacefulness that sighs inaudibly beneath, through, within the clamor of the landscape. All about me are verdant seas of fern, wooded glens, small random hamlets, shepherds climbing and farm girls calling after their dogs and sheep.
[12 July 1940]

A Welsh Hundred: Glimpses of Life in Wales
drawn from a pair of family diaries for 1841 and 1940

1.
THE FARAWAY PARADISE
BY WILLIAM BEBB
compiled & edited by W. Ambrose Bebb
M.A. Lecturer/Reader in the Normal College, Bangor, Wales
originally published October 1941

2.
1940:
GLEANINGS FROM A DIARY
by W. Ambrose Bebb
originally published February 1941

translated by
Marc K. Stengel
2008

AuthorHouse™
1663 Liberty Drive, Suite 200
Bloomington, IN 47403
www.authorhouse.com
Phone: 1-800-839-8640

These works were originally published in Welsh in 1941 by Llyfrau'r Dryw *[Wren Books], later part of Christopher Davies Publishers, Ltd.*

All Rights Reserved
Original works: © *1955 Estate of W. Ambrose Bebb*
English translation: © *2009 Marc K. Stengel*

No part of this book may be reproduced, stored in a retrieval system or transmitted by any means without the written permission of the copyright holders.

This edition first published by AuthorHouse 7/3/09

ISBN: 978-1-4343-5991-9 (sc)

Library of Congress Control Number: 2008906877

Printed in the United States of America
Bloomington, Indiana

This book is printed on acid-free paper.

*On the summit of one of the farthest ridges, I can make out the tiny village of Darowen
smiling down at me affectionately amidst a raiment of white and green. The soft
shapeliness of the mountain known as Aran Fawddwy muses in silence
beneath a billowing shroud of mist.*
[12 July 1940]

*A bomb has fallen somewhere! ... A boom of thunder follows a moment later. Above the
long streak of random flashes, three, then four great disks of light stand still. Then they
start expanding and moving towards us, swaying as they approach.
They're like the awful, seething eyes of a giant.*
[25 September 1940]

*...A lusty beer before the fire
And a lissome lass for loving.*
[24 October 1940]

*A diary? Why, the very premise of a diary is selfishness itself –
even more so the decision to publish one.*
[*Epilogue*, 1940: Gleanings from a Diary]

Dedication

I fy ngwraig i,
Terry

Contents

Foreword
- Translator's Foreword — xi
- Notes to Translator's Foreword — xxxiii
- Acknowledgments — xxxvii
- Regarding Endnotes — xxxix

Book I
- The Faraway Paradise — 1
  - About the Book — 3
  - Author's Dedication — 5
  - Map — 7
  - Preface — 9
  - The Faraway Paradise — 15
  - Notes — 73

Book II
- 1940: Gleanings from a Diary — 81
  - About the Book — 83
  - Author's Dedication — 85
  - Map — 87
  - Preface — 89
  - 1940: Gleanings from a Diary — 91
  - Notes — 169

Index — 179

About the Author — 189

About the Translator — 191

Translator's Foreword

In more than one sense, the two diaries that have been combined into this compact single volume are like ghosts. As revenants, they are re-appearing in 2009 from beyond the grave for out-of-print books, to which they were consigned almost 70 years ago after their well received initial publications in 1941. As poltergeists, they are barging into the English-language world for the first time – brash upstarts and the presumptuous brain-children of a translator who has literally willed them into being in defiance of apathy towards the unfamiliar on the one hand, the logic of the marketplace on the other. But illogicality is the poltergeist's favorite mischief in any event.

Most ghostly of all, perhaps, is the relationship that has arisen between the deceased author of these diaries-made-public and his very much alive translator, who has intruded himself into them uninvited. Although separated by time, distance and language, both men have established an intimate bond that the two of them – bold as it is to assert – have shared equally in forging.

William Ambrose Bebb, born in 1894, was roughly of the same generation as my grandparents. When he died in 1955, I was still a year from being born; and we would still not meet – in the figurative sense, of course – until I determined in 2005 to translate into English a selection of his entertaining and unconventional works concerning the history of Wales. As it happened, I had only recently been alerted to their existence by the merest passing reference to one of them in a footnote by the late historian Sir Rees R. Davies. In a general acknowledgment of sources consulted during his writing of *The Revolt of Owain Glyn Dŵr*, Davies wrote, "A charming and undervalued portrait of Welsh society based on the evidence of the poetry is W. Ambrose Bebb, *Machlud yr Oesoedd Canol* [*Twilight of the Middle Ages*] (Swansea, 1951)."[1]

A juxtaposition of the words "charming" and "undervalued" has an electrifying effect upon some people. In my own case, the charge was sufficient to goad me into finding, then translating this book for the first time into English (publication forthcoming). It was clear to me then, is even clearer now, that here was a unique, idiosyncratic, uncompromising voice which was, on account of the author's deliberate intent, entirely mute within the English-language world. (Bebb could be emphatic on this score: "My dear friend!" he once fretted to a Breton-speaking acquaintance who lapsed too frequently into French; "Neither my wife nor I speak a word of English – *ever* – to our children. And still, their English is none the worse for it."[2] The Breton language is remarkably similar, and is of course related, to Welsh.)

And yet after translating seven of Bebb's histories, all of which will be published in due course, I concluded that his strictly academic histories concerning various periods and aspects of life in Wales were too specialized and narrowly focused to serve as compelling introductions – in English – to the wit, vivacity and piquancy of Bebb's prose and personality. But among his standard histories there also exist several diaries in the writer's hand; and two of these in particular seemed ideal for putting Bebb's best foot forward in an English-language debut.

The first diary selected, *The Faraway Paradise*, is Bebb's historical-fictional reconstruction of a year, 1841, in the life of his great-great-uncle William Bebb, who lived in rural Montgomeryshire in the middle of Wales near Llanbrynmair, east of Machynlleth. The second book, *1940: Gleanings from a Diary*, is Bebb's eye-witness account of the first full year of the Second World War, with its dreadful losses in Continental Europe and terrifying consequences for Great Britain. By choosing to compile these two diaries under the title *A Welsh Hundred* I am, of course, evoking Wales' ancient territorial division known as *y cantref* – "the hundred" (literally, "one hundred farmsteads"), a subdivision of county or shire lands. More significantly, however, as bookends for a century that witnessed profound transformations in the only Principality of a far-flung British Empire, Bebb's pair of diaries serve as an enchanting, provocative introduction to the life and spirit of a Wales that most English speakers outside of that small country simply know nothing about.

Part of the immense pleasure in composing these translations was coming to terms – literally – with a gorgeous language that nevertheless can baffle an inelastic, English-comprehending mind. Then too there was the delight in coming to more figurative terms with a man praised by his peers as "the writer of the most beautiful and most vivacious Welsh of our century"[3] and "as a literary man [who] was a splendid artist. He had the rich vocabulary of Cardiganshire,... of dialect witticism, moral idioms, proverbs and rhymes, a cascade of language."[4] Bebb's personality – and by extension, his genuinely Welsh perspective upon life in this world – is on fascinating display in expressions like "without hairs on his tongue" (i.e., without mincing words); "day draws its head in" (the days are shortening); "might as well put the fiddle on the roof" (throw in the towel); and "what's wrong with the cheese?" (what gives?).

In both diaries, Bebb manages to convey vividly the rounded wholeness of life in a Wales that manages to participate fully in a global community of nations while yet persevering as a comprehensive culture that is traditional, somewhat exotic, unmistakably *sui generis*. As his colleague and friend Saunders Lewis observed on the occasion of Bebb's untimely death at age 61, "he could describe men better than cities; villages better than mighty towns; fields and tillage and the color and scent of the earth better than architecture.... The description of the farmstead of his childhood at the beginning of *Crwydro'r Cyfandir* [*Roaming the Continent*]...is a key to his entire body of work."[5]

Lewis' perception is apt. In the chapter of the travel book that Lewis cites, Bebb has just returned home after several years of studying and teaching at Rennes in Brittany and at the Sorbonne in Paris. While climbing up to the Banc, as the high pasture of his parents' farm was known, he exults with a tinge of irony, "Let the reader bear in mind that there isn't the slightest connection between this place-name and that institution where cautious folk of this day and age keep all their silver and gold." Wealth is where you find – and enjoy – it after all. Upon reaching his high, familiar perch Bebb points out the "three glories of the Banc": The first is its commanding vistas over the surrounding countryside, from the peak of Pumlumon to the town of Lampeter to the shores of Lake Eiddwen. The second delight is a little stream that flows through the middle of the Banc. It issues from an ever-dependable mountain tarn above; and its clear, cool waters have been known to soothe many a sore limb fatigued by hiking and climbing.

"And the third glory is the teeming acres of ferns that grow to remarkable heights upon the Banc, a sort of forest of fronds. If you ever want to get completely lost, here's the place to do so. I've been known to walk through them for long stretches, forging my way with ample difficulty, all the while pondering the branches that reach so high above my head and fill my nostrils with their perfume. After a while in their midst, you feel as if your very heart and soul have been christened by them. And it's not until you experience this sensation during each and every visit that you will finally possess the keys to the virtue and genius of this place. Then, when that happens, you and the thicket of bracken become one – laughing together, soaking up the same delight of a sunny day, drenching in the same downpour of a storm sweeping up from the fens of Cors Caron."[6]

In both diaries as well, Bebb uses glittering set-pieces like this one to punctuate a year of travails and frustrations. Against its 19th-century backdrop of political unrest, Chartism,[7] religious debate, financial insecurity and the emigration of friends and neighbors to America, *The Faraway Paradise* also crackles with William Bebb's evocative descriptions of, for example, a mighty mountain tempest in early spring or of harvest-time and market days in autumn. A century later, in *1940*, W. Ambrose Bebb's Easter hike in Snowdonia; July visit to Ysbyty Ifan; and September labors at the grain harvest all serve as potent analgesics against the news and experience of war.

In concluding his elegy upon the death of his friend Ambrose Bebb, Saunders Lewis wrote, "One can hear his voice in the page-leaves of his books. Alas, one will not hear it otherwise from now on."[8] If Lewis intended by this to put Bebb's memory elegantly to rest, he would perhaps have been surprised at how far his friend's voice has carried in both time and distance. For there is an element in my own deepening collaboration with Bebb that neither the late writer himself nor Lewis – nor I – could possibly have foreseen. Among the Welsh-speaking Welsh – *Y Cymry Cymraeg* – Bebb was known during his lifetime as a great teacher, writer, speaker: "He was grand without being grandiose," one of his former students is reported to have said in Robin Chapman's biography.[9] But above all, Bebb is still remembered in Welsh Wales today as one of a trio of founders, with Saunders Lewis and G.J. Williams, of *Y Mudiad Cymreig* [The Welsh Movement] which eventually became the *Plaid Cymru* [Party of Wales] of contemporary politics in both the United Kingdom Parliament and in the much newer Welsh Assembly. The English-speaking world is, by and large, unaware of this; and a native Englishman in particular would be hard-pressed to find any significance in this circumstance anyway. The same could be said about Bebb's voluminous literary production – indeed, about Welsh prose and poetry in general. "Wales has a major literature," one contemporary commentator has observed, "that has tragically no voice in twentieth-century Britain as a whole"[10] – or, it might be said, in twenty-first-century Britain either.

But here is where Lewis may have been a bit too hasty to close the covers on the page-leaves of his friend. For me, a native of the American South, whose hometown of Nashville, Tennessee, witnessed the founding of the Fugitive/Agrarian movement at Vanderbilt University in the 1920s and '30s, it is not only Bebb's books that have provoked a fascination with this curious Welshman but also the striking harmony of his politics with that of the Tennessee Agrarians. The similarities between a Welsh nationalist movement and a Southern U.S. regionalist movement are all the more striking and unanticipated because, despite their patent sympathies in points of view, despite their corresponding vulnerabilities at the hands of political rivals, these two influential groups would surely have been mutually unaware of one another. Certainly, the Southerners would have despaired of comprehending Welsh; whereas the Welshmen, who generally knew but pointedly abjured English, would have little countenanced Tennessee. To co-opt the wonderment that Salman Rushdie recently expressed about Mughal India and Renaissance Italy in his most recent novel *The Enchantress of Florence*: "How interesting it is that two apparently separate cultures should, within half a century of each other, have been coming up with the same notions without conferring."[11]

A detailed examination of the convergence of Welsh Nationalist and Southern Agrarian philosophies is beyond the scope or purpose of this Foreword; but perhaps some examples of their affinities will whet an appetite that can be sated in future: In Wales during the '20s and '30s of the last century, Bebb and his fellow partisans championed *gwlad, gwerin* and *iaith* [countryside, common folk and language]. During those decades, in fact, there was something pan-Celtic in the air that gravitated naturally towards rural and agrarian preoccupations – and away from the urban, industrial and imperial ones associated with the horrors and aftermath of The Great War of 1914-18. In Ireland, George William Russell (known as "Æ" to his friends James Joyce and W.B. Yeats) wrote frequently in defense of rural sensibilities for the journal he edited, *The Irish Homestead*. "I would regret with a personal passion," he wrote in an open letter "To Irish Farmers" in 1915, "that your class should cease to be predominant in our national life. I believe that country is happiest and has the most moral and stable life where agriculture predominates among the industries. A fine life is possible for humanity working on the land, bronzed by the sun and wind, living close to nature, affected by its arcane influences, which bring about essential depth and a noble simplicity of character. To create a rural civilization is a great ideal.

"There is another life, fine in its way, where humanity, collected in the cities, has exalted urban civilization by the arts and sciences until the cities are beautiful and healthy and the life is quickened by intellect. The first civilization it is in our power to create in a generation at its best. The second for us would indeed be a long labor,…but we will move a hundred times more rapidly to national prosperity and happiness if we try to make our civilization predominantly rural."[12]

Sentiments like these, it should be noted, made a profound impression upon one of Bebb's close associates, D.J. Williams, whose 1929 chapbook *A.E. a Chymru* [*A.E. and Wales*] meant to adapt Russell's brand of Irish agrarianism to a Welsh intellectual climate. "Agriculture is the foundation of man's stewardship of the world," Williams wrote. "Life has no future in the great cities, according to A.E.... In them, one finds only dust and ashes. For life at its fullest – in all its fecundity, its flowering, its maturing and ripening – only the countryside will do. And this must be preserved."[13] Williams proceeded to quote A.E. directly: "'As Walt Whitman has said, wherever men and women live life at its best, there you will find a great metropolis – even if it is nothing more than a humble hamlet. One of the mistakes of thinking only in material terms is to suppose that one cannot enjoy the same high standards of living in a village that one finds in a proper town.'"[14] Williams seemed to be echoing Bebb's own sentiments when he declared, "I do indeed believe that A.E.'s spiritual philosophy as well as his practical recommendations for transforming that philosophy into social reality constitute invaluable advice that we cannot afford to ignore at this point in history."[15] And in fact, in the following diary entry for 1 June 1841, Bebb's alter ego William says as much for himself: "If agriculture dies, ...it will be the *death of talent, the death of excellence, the death of every rural art*. The sweet sounds that fill even the smallest villages with harmony will fade away. Those noises and activities interwoven into the pattern of a Welshman's life – that actually collude in supporting and maintaining Welsh Society – all of them will be dead and gone."[16]

Apart from his concerted efforts spent in championing the virtues of village and small-farm life – even from his perch as lecturer in Welsh and History at Normal College in Bangor, Wales – our diarist

Glimpses of Life in Wales

also witnessed and sympathized with like-minded gestures in Brittany devoted to similar ideals. In his 1939 account of a political meeting in the northern Breton town of Tréguier on the eve of yet another world war, Bebb noted that a Mme Drouart "discussed ways of keeping the Bretons on the land, of enticing them to forego the cities and re-emphasize their Breton origins. She suggested ways for giving them their dignity back; for making them conscious of their forefathers' inheritance; for binding them to their homesteads with invisible bonds of tradition, custom, ritual. She encouraged them to build their own homes in the native styles of their land, with handsome furnishings showcasing traditional craftsmanship. She meant for them to learn their language again, the history of their nation, their literature and folk wisdom – and to cultivate a sense of duty, honor and justice. She might as well have been addressing one of the meetings of the Nationalist Party of Wales...."[17]

During this same inter-war period, albeit on the opposite side of the Atlantic, the fledgling Vanderbilt group of Agrarians were likewise preoccupied with regionalism, tradition and literature in the American South. Their provocative manifesto *I'll Take My Stand: The South and the Agrarian Tradition* was first published in 1930. Donald Davidson, one of the most vehement of the book's contributors, insisted in a later essay that "our literature, architecture, folk-lore, history, accent dissolve the national complex into sectional entities. Rivers, mountain ranges, deserts, degrees of latitude, differences of soil and climate divide us."[18] Even in an essay sharply critical of Agrarianism as realistic economic policy, Robert B. Downs of the University of Illinois ascribed a wishful idealism to *I'll Take My Stand*: "In the lead essay, 'Reconstructed but Unregenerate,'...by [John Crowe] Ransom, the claim is made that Southern culture was built upon 'European principles,' the chief features of which are to encourage the right relations with nature and one's fellow men, to respect leisure, and to devote energy to 'the free life of the mind.' Following the European example, the Old South had enjoyed 'the social arts of dress, conversation, manners, the table, the hunt, politics, oratory and the pulpit.' Ransom acknowledged that a certain amount of industrialism was inevitable, for the sake of the region's prosperity, but that it should be kept within strict bounds. The South should reject blatant materialism, noisy salesmanship, and dollar-chasing. Instead, it should unite with Western agrarians to work for the preservation of rural life in America."[19]

When Bebb addressed his party, *Plaid Cymru*, in 1942 on the topic of "What Sort of Wales Will We Have?" he declared that *his* ideal was a "Welsh-speaking Wales of free, Christian yeomanry – whose faith is most cherished of all."[20] He might well have cribbed his notes from *I'll Take My Stand*, in which Ransom had written, "The agrarian discontent in America is deeply grounded in the love of the tiller of the soil, which is probably, it must be confessed, not peculiar to the Southern specimen but one of the more ineradicable human attachments.... He identifies himself with a spot on the ground, and this ground carries a good deal of meaning; it defines itself for him as nature."[21]

Throughout Bebb's writings is an admiration for the *gwerin* and the *tyddynnwr* [common folk and free-hold, yeoman farmer] who serve unwittingly as bulwarks against dehumanizing trends in modern life, language and culture. When Allen Tate, the poet, critic and a fellow contributor to *I'll Take My Stand*, observed that modern compulsions have "destroyed our regional societies," he appears to have been "channeling" W. Ambrose Bebb. "In the West," Tate continued, "our peculiar civilization was based upon regional autonomy.... Man belonged to his village, valley, mountain or seacoast;...[but] regionalism without civilization – which means, with us, regionalism without classical Christian culture – becomes provincialism. For provincialism is that state of mind in which regional men lose their origins in the past and its continuity into the present, and begin every day as if there were no yesterday."[22]

It is crucially important for an English-speaker to bear in mind that the possibility of "no yesterday" is simply untenable within the world-view of Welsh-speaking Wales. In his series of historical works, Bebb makes it abundantly clear that he couldn't have agreed more with the assertion – restated recently by Jason Walford Davies – that Wales and its language constitute "the oldest living poetic tradition in Europe."[23] In his diary *1940*, Bebb deplored the barbarian assault that Germany was waging against France – a cultural heiress of Rome and, to Bebb's way of thinking, half-sister to the Wales that Rome had civilized even before Gaul, nearly two millennia ago: "My darling Paris, city of cities, literary paradise, cradle of culture for the last several centuries, blessed daughter of humanity – you are in mortal danger. The barbarians are at your walls; the savage is at your gates…. [M]y breast heaves with all these overwhelming thoughts and feelings of grief for Paris' unmerciful fate."[24]

It is remarkable the extent to which the self-images of some Vanderbilt Agrarians parallel those of Bebb and his Welsh compatriots. In a letter dated 10 August 1929, from Concarneau, Brittany, Allen Tate spelled out to Donald Davidson his conviction that the success of their Agrarian project depended upon strict adherence to "its prototype – the historical social and religious scheme of Europe. We may be the last Europeans – there being no Europeans in Europe at present."[25] By a remarkable coincidence, 10 years later to the month (31 August, in fact), Bebb would himself be in Concarneau stumping in the Welsh and Breton vernaculars for Agrarian-like reforms, even while louring clouds of war gathered overhead.

As the two Bebb diaries compiled in this volume make positively clear – to say nothing of the writer's academic histories – the continuity of Welsh history is a resounding, hallowed theme. So too are the inevitability of tragedy and its annealing effect upon national character. As every student of "Welshness" knows, the first major work written in the native Welsh language of the British Isles was *Y Gododdin*. Titled after a long-vanished Brythonic tribe of the same name, the poem is a celebration of the martial ethos for a people who considered themselves directly descended from Aeneas of Troy's great-grandson, Brutus – hence Britain (*Prydain* in Welsh), land of Brutus. But unlike the victorious Achaeans of Homer's *Iliad*, the 300 warriors of *Y Gododdin* who rode into battle sometime around 600 AD were obliterated by Saxon adversaries. Aside from the bard Aneurin who lived to tell the tale, only one (or perhaps three) of these proto-Welsh knights survived amongst their fellow fallen *marchogion*. Almost 700 years later, in 1282, *Llywellyn ein Llyw Olaf* [Llywelyn our Last Ruler] succumbed to another Germanic invader, the Plantagenet heir and Anglo-Norman warlord Edward I "Longshanks." Even so, dreams of an independent Wales would not expire – or merely slip into hibernation perhaps – until the princely outlaw Owain Glyn Dŵr [Glendower, to Shakespeare's ear] was finally put to rout in 1413.

The American South, of course, has been bedeviled by her own Lost Cause in the aftermath of defeat in The Civil War of 1861-65. For the likes of Davidson, memories of the Lost Cause were both proximate and personal. It was his grandmother, after all, "who in the [Eighteen-]Sixties had seen her boy-friends captured by marauding Federal soldiers and shot in cold blood on the main street of her home town."[26] The way novelist, poet-laureate and *I'll Take My Stand* co-contributor Robert Penn Warren once parsed the Lost Cause is striking for its unintentional resonance with Welsh sensibility: "The South has one peculiarity: it was a nation once, and that makes a vast difference, though it can be forgotten that it makes a difference. Another thing that's forgotten that makes a difference is that southerners felt that they had created the Union – Washington and Jefferson [both Virginians] had created the Union – and the North was going to take it away from them."[27] By way of comparison, it is still a given in Welsh Wales that England, also, arrogated to herself what the sons of Brutus had originally bestowed upon British posterity.

But according to the analysis of *Sewanee Review* editor George Core, himself an alumnus of Vanderbilt University, it was Tate who most clearly perceived the mythic dimension of the South's exceptionalism, the poignancy of her Lost Cause: "'There was a sort of unity of feeling, of which we were not then very much aware,' [Tate] has written, 'which came out of – to give it a big name – a common historical myth.' ...[Tate] has defined it as the Greco-Trojan myth – 'Northerners as the upstart Greeks, Southerners as the older, more civilized Trojans' – saying of myth in general that it is 'a dramatic projection of heroic action, or of the tragic failure of heroic action, upon the reality of the common life of a society, so that the myth *is* the reality.'

"Tate goes on to say that he sees the southern myth along these lines: 'The South, afflicted with the curse of slavery – a curse, like that of Original Sin, for which no single person is responsible – has to be destroyed, the good along with the evil. The old order had a great deal of good, one of the "goods" being a result of the evil; for slavery itself entailed a certain moral responsibility.... This old order, in which the good could not be salvaged from the bad, was replaced by a new order which was in many ways worse than the old.'"[28]

The weight of the past continues to bear down painfully upon both Bebb's and the Agrarians' posthumous reputations. As the diary *1940* boldly if naïvely intimates, it was (and remains) possible to say awkward things and to favor errant causes without benefit of hindsight. Torn between personal loyalties and philosophical principle, Bebb wounded his future reputation by sympathizing with rank causes like the royalist militancy of Charles Maurras' *Action Française*. Bebb also espoused wishful thinking and benefit-of-the-doubt opinions about Mussolini. The Agrarians, likewise, have ever been plagued by accusations – generally creditable – of segregationist tendencies in racial matters and idealist elitism in their social-economic prescriptions. Tate even went so far on one occasion as to propose to his fellow Agrarian, novelist Andrew Lytle, that the Agrarian movement "should emerge from 'a society something like the *Action Française* group,'... [even though Tate] had lost 'sympathy with all designs merely to restore the ruins'" of the antebellum Old South.[29]

In the view of historian C. Vann Woodward, moreover, it was Tate who suggested "that after the First World War the South arrived at a crossroads of history where an old traditional order was being rapidly obliterated and a new modern order was being simultaneously brought to birth. Caught at these crossroads, the Southerner was made more keenly conscious at once of the present and of the past. His sensitivity to the current change heightened his awareness of past differences, and his intensified remembrance of things past added corresponding poignancy to his awareness of things present. As Tate put it, 'that backward glance gave us the Southern renascence, a literature conscious of the past in the present.'"[30]

But surely there is a deeply subconscious element at work as well, in both these Welsh and these Southern personalities. "To be the object of contempt or patronizing tolerance on the part of proud neighbors," the late philosopher-historian Sir Isaiah Berlin has written, "is one of the most traumatic experiences that individuals or societies can suffer. The response, as often as not, is pathological exaggeration of one's real or imaginary virtues, and resentment and hostility towards the proud, the happy, the successful.... Those who cannot boast of great political, military or economic achievements, or a magnificent tradition of art or thought, seek comfort and strength in the notion of the free and creative life of the spirit within them, uncorrupted by the vices of power or sophistication."[31] Ostensibly, Berlin was discussing the rise of militant nationalism – Nazism – in Germany between two world wars. But it is more than a little bracing to sense how aptly this analysis also fits certain behaviors and attitudes in both Wales and the American South during that same inter-war period.

In my own outsider's opinion, Bebb's flirtation with Maurras' reactionary monarchism and the Agrarians' distinctly *un*modern perceptions of race relations are feet-of-clay reminders of universal human fallibility. They serve to emphasize the quandaries and frustrations of writers and thinkers on both sides of the Atlantic whose love for Wales and for The South, respectively, forced difficult choices upon them "against a backdrop of unspeakable horrors"[32] in the receding ebb-tide of one world war and the incoming flood-tide of a next one.

To this day, moreover, it must be borne in mind that Bebb broke with the party he co-founded because his insistence that Hitler be stopped could in no way be reconciled with his party's official declaration of pacifist neutrality – even within a nominally *United Kingdom*. As D. Hywel Davies recounts in his history of the formative years of *Plaid Cymru*, "Ambrose Bebb, one of the Nationalist Party's founding fathers, withdrew his support in 1939 in protest against its anti-war policy. Nazi Germany, in his view, had to be destroyed."[33] Bebb himself could not have been more plain-spoken about this, for in his diary entry for 24 February 1940, he declared: "And though I have little sympathy with England, and none at all with her attempt to hold herself blameless, I do believe that a German victory would represent the utmost misfortune, even for us in Wales."[34] "On this score, I am compelled to disagree with my colleagues in Wales."[35]

If, however, it were necessary to pass judgment upon Bebb's conception of nationalism and the Vanderbilt Agrarians' understanding of regionalism, one would have to say they overreached themselves. For all their pretensions to statecraft and social-economic policy, they were at root literary men – *llenorion* in the Welsh – poets and novelists, historians and writers, a diarist. And according to one of their kindred spirits, the Anglo-Welsh poet David Jones, "it is the business of a poet in the sixth, or eighteenth, or any century, to express the dilemma, not to comment upon it, or pretend to a solution."[36] From this, it is not a particularly long or difficult step to Socrates' own opinion on the matter: "The question is…not whether or not there are good men…or whether there have been in past time, but whether virtue can be taught. It amounts to the question whether the good men of this and former times have known how to hand on to someone else the goodness that was in themselves, or whether on the contrary it is not something that can be handed over, or that one man can receive from another."[37]

Perhaps it seems over-bleak to suggest that description, not prescription, is the proper responsibility of *llenorion* – be they Welsh or Agrarian, British or American. But if this is so, isn't it also worth pondering whether persuasion is preferable to insistence? In George Core's view, for example, "the [Agrarian] movement succeeded brilliantly on the plane of ideas, but failed dismally on the plane of action." Just the same, "the Agrarians were among the first literate and vocal ecologists in the United States."[38] And as for Bebb's own dedication to the cause of *y gwerin* and *y wlad* [the common people and the land] – which he evokes so movingly in the pair of diaries that follow – his views now seem remarkably prophetic in light of contemporary British developments. As recently as 2008, for example, the *Daily Telegraph* newspaper in London – underneath the headline "Our Countryside in Peril" – observed that "there seems to have occurred an alarming change in our national attitude, away from our agrarian roots.... Whole communities are being swept away,...undermining the ancient, rural foundations of British civil society."[39]

Contrary to modern intuition – chastened as *that* has been by a 20th century full of nationalist-bred agonies – one suggested response to the deterioration of "British civil society" seems curiously anachronistic. "Nationalism is a potent, visceral force," writes the arch-Unionist and British conservative commentator Simon Heffer. "Denying it is like denying human nature."[40] Heffer argues, surprisingly yet convincingly (even "presciently" according to *The Spectator* of 19 April 2008), for a modern expression of *English* – rather than *British* – self-consciousness in the form of "an English nationalist party"[41] analogous to Bebb's *Plaid Cymru* in Wales. He proposes that "the civilized and educated classes who have so long repudiated and cringed at the very idea of nationalism can take a hand in creating a more acceptable form of it themselves."[42] As if in posthumous reply, Isaiah Berlin himself cries out, "Who, in the nineteenth century, would have predicted the rise of acute nationalism in Canada, in Pakistan (indeed, the very possibility of Pakistan itself would have met with considerable skepticism among Indian nationalist leaders a hundred years ago), or in Wales or Brittany or Scotland or the Basque country?"[43]

But perhaps Heffer's cheek is less audacious than modern "received opinion" dare admit. He and Bebb are in quite good, even august company, it turns out. Writing in the last quarter of the 18th century, at a time of revolutionary ferment in the West when old allegiances were being severed and ancient dominations shattered, the philosopher Johann Gottfried von Herder was calmly championing a "distinctive-but-equal" cohabitation among disparate societies. As the present-day historian Walter Russell Mead has recently observed, "Herder did not believe that people could, should, or would 'overcome' their cultural differences over time.... Instead, he believed that the diversity of perspectives would persist and deepen as humanity moved toward the culmination of history. His vision of the end of history was not of a human community sharing a single culture and set of institutions, but of a family of different and sometimes competing perceptions and ideas."[44]

Appropriately enough where Bebb's language-dominated nationalism is concerned, Herder was convinced that "each national language forms itself in accordance with the ethics and manner of thought of its people.... Each head who thinks for itself will also speak for himself, and so his manner of expression gets formed in his own way too: he will impress on his language characteristic features of his manner of seeing and characteristic features of the weaknesses and virtues of his manner of thought...."[45] Mead puts it more epigrammatically: "Those who speak different languages don't just use different words; they see different things."[46]

Revealing a few of these different things happens to be the express justification for introducing the following two Welsh diaries to English readers for the first time. Clearly Bebb's nationalism is a different thing from Heffer's nationalism. Bebb's agrarianism is also a different thing from Davidson's Agrarianism. Still, as D.J. Williams observed, "it's surprising to consider how much similarity of human nature there is in every age and in every country. Only superficially are there any apparent differences."[47] Perhaps that's why Salman Rushdie, as noted above, was careful to express his own curiosity – but certainly no surprise – in the similarities he has found between "apparently separated cultures" of the East and West. The celebrated 20th-century theologian Reinhold Niebuhr undoubtedly wished more people could react this same way: "The brutalities of social conflict" could be abolished, he wrote rather dejectedly in 1932, "only if human groups, whether racial, national or economic, could achieve a degree of reason and sympathy which would permit them to see and to understand the interests of others as vividly as they understand their own, and a moral goodwill which would prompt them to affirm the rights of others as vigorously as they affirm their own. Given the inevitable limitations of human nature and the limits of the human imagination and intelligence, this is an ideal which individuals may approximate but which is beyond the capacities of human societies."[48]

Viewed through a lens of this sort, the following pages of Bebb's diaries bring into focus the idea that the pangs of recognizing – of experiencing first-hand – the loss of a way of life are equally as sharp in Welsh as in English. And the absence of a remedial prescription is equally poignant and rending whether one happens to be British or American. Bebb happened to be expert at "expressing the dilemma" of these circumstances in his portraits of two different years in Wales, exactly one century apart. He has tactfully left it to his readers, however, to "pretend to a solution."

• • • • •

It was the Romans who attributed to the Celtic Brythons – predecessors of *Y Cymry*, the Welsh – a belief in an afterlife. It amuses me to ponder what W. Ambrose Bebb, from a celestial perch this time, would think about a post-Agrarian Southerner in the United States manhandling his prose, unbidden, into the English language he foreswore. He must be smiling, to be sure; otherwise the work could not have gone so well or been so personally rewarding.

In his essay upon the Anglo-Welsh poetry of Anglican vicar R.S. Thomas, the writer and translator Jason Walford Davies succeeds in revealing the primal terror that envelops every would-be translator: "Failing to understand a language is an excellent metaphor for going out of earshot of God."[49] As if to test my mettle even further, the great R.S. himself (the "Ogre of Wales" as his own parishioners perceived him) has roared, "When something as poetic as this land of hills and streams is concerned, I have no interest in translation."[50] "If anyone believes he can taste Welshness without the language, he deceives himself. Every mountain and stream, every farm and lane announces to the world that landscape in Wales is something more."[51]

I dare not defy these my betters; but I have proceeded with my translations in spite of the warnings, and in Thomas' case, in spite of his Jovian thunderings. Naïvely, and in a manner insufficiently deferential perhaps, I have simply wanted to share the Wales of W. Ambrose Bebb with my friends as well as with fellow strangers, like myself, to the Welsh language. In so doing, I have come to appreciate the responsibility that accrues to every translation, insofar as "translation is not a simple transfer."[52] It is, instead, a sort of journey of interpretation in which there are ample opportunities for losing one's bearings altogether. If I have been spared this dismal outcome, it is the guiding hand of Fortune I have to thank. For as my own curiosity grew about correspondences between Bebb's Wales and my South, I found myself pleasantly surprised – edified even – by the realization that "one way of dealing with the unknown is to associate it with something one already knows; the new is mapped in terms of established norms, analogies are forced, differences are reduced and conventional associations work to deconstruct."[53] The South I know from the inside, in other words, has helped me intuit the Wales I know only as an outsider. And once I'd become helplessly enthralled to this daunting and presumptive enterprise, I drew special reinforcement from the sanguine Stoicism expressed by Irish poet and translator Thomas Kinsella: "I think that the human function is to elicit order from experience, to detect the significant substance of our individual and common pasts and translate it imaginatively, scientifically, bodily into an ever more coherent and capacious entity – or to try to do so until we fail."[54]

So if the best of a Welsh landscape cannot truly be translated, perhaps it can at least be verbally mapped, then mined for the significant substance of shared human experience. Accordingly, where Bebb's two diaries are concerned my principal aim has merely been to indicate the proper directions to and relative distances between the notable landmarks of this author's evocative Welsh prose. This is all I have intended to do; and I hope I have succeeded at least in part, with a minimum of misdirection or wrong turns of phrase.

When he died, yet another of Bebb's friends and colleagues elegized him with plain-spoken candor: "He had the gentleness of the Montgomery region of his ancestors; the tenacity of the Cardiganshire that he adopted. He was flexible and accommodating with people, inflexible and resolute on matters of conviction. He never betrayed a principle to save face; and he was an untiring worker who yet made time for everyone who called upon him.... He was a seeker after his country's past and a builder of her future.... He was a Welshman with no deceit to his name and honest to a fault. It was easy indeed to like him."[55]

It is easy still. And I am grateful to Mr. Bebb's family – particularly to his youngest son Ifan – and to his former publishers, *Llyfrau'r Dryw* [Wren Books, now Christopher Davies Publishers, Ltd.] for the generous permissions they have extended that allow me to submit Mr. W. Ambrose Bebb's *A Welsh Hundred* to an English-reading audience for the first time, with compliments humble yet sincere.

Marc K. Stengel

Nashville, Tennessee, *yr Unol Daleithiau*

Beltân; Calan Mai 2008

Notes to Translator's Foreword

1. R.R. Davies, *The Revolt of Owain Glyn Dŵr* (Oxford U. Press, 1997), p. 343.
2. W. A. Bebb, *Dydd-Lyfr Pythefnos, neu Y Ddawns Angau* [*A Fortnight's Diary, or The Dance of Death*] (Sackville Printing Works, 1939), p. 82.
3. Gareth Meils (André Morgan, trans.), "Ambrose Bebb," *Planet*, no. 37/38 (1977), p. 73.
4. Saunders Lewis, *Yr Argyfwng* [*The Crisis*] (*Llyfrau'r Dryw* [Wren Books], 1956), p. 12; cited by Gareth Meils, *ibid.*, p. 77.
5. Lewis, *ibid.*, p. 12.
6. W. A. Bebb, *Crwydro'r Cyfandir* [*Roaming the Continent*] (Hughes a'i Fab [Hughes and Son], 1936), pp. 22-23.
7. A working-class movement which, in 1838, promulgated a six-point Charter that stipulated universal male suffrage; secret balloting; annual elections; equal electoral districts; stipends for Members of Parliament; and no property requirements to stand for election. The Chartist movement eventually failed, although most of its aims have ultimately been achieved. (Source: *The Cambridge Historical Encyclopedia of Great Britain and Ireland*)
8. Saunders Lewis, *op. cit.*, p 13.
9. Robin Chapman, *W. Ambrose Bebb* (Gwasg Prifysgol Cymru [University of Wales Press], 1997), p. 129.

10. Jason Walford Davies, "'Thick Ambush of Shadows': Allusions to Welsh literature in the work of R.S. Thomas," *Welsh Writing in English: A Yearbook of Critical Essays 1* (New Welsh Review, 1995), p. 77.
11. Salman Rushdie to Matthew d'Ancona, "'We have been wimpish about defending our ideas,'" *The Spectator* (12 April 2008), p. 20.
12. G.W. Russell, "Ireland, Agriculture and the War; February 20, 1915," *Selections from the Contributions to* THE IRISH HOMESTEAD *by G.W. Russell – A.E., Vol. I* [Henry Summerfield, ed.] (Humanities Press, 1978), p. 451.
13. D.J. Williams, *A.E. a Chymru* [*A.E. and Wales*] (*Gwasg Aberystwyth* [Aberystwyth Press], 1929), p. 27.
14. *Ibid.*, p. 28.
15. *Ibid.*, p. 40.
16. W. A. Bebb, *Y Baradwys Bell* [*The Faraway Paradise*] (*Llyfrau'r Dryw* [Wren Books], 1941), pp. 39.
17. *Dydd-Lyfr Pythefnos*, *op. cit.*, p. 33.
18. Donald Davidson, "Sectionalism in the United States," *Hound & Horn* (No. 6, July-September 1933), pp. 588; cited in *Tennessee Historical Quarterly* (Vol. LV, No. 3; Fall 1996), pp. 262-263.
19. Robert B. Downs, *Books that Changed the South* (University of North Carolina Press, 1977), p. 231.
20. Chapman, *op. cit.*, p. 133.
21. John Crowe Ransom, "Reconstructed but Unregenerate," *I'll Take My Stand* (Harper Torchbook, 1962), pp. 18, 19-20.
22. Allen Tate, "The New Provincialism," *Essays of Four Decades*. (ISI Books, 1999), pp. 542, 545.
23. J.W. Davies, *op. cit.*, p 103.
24. W.A. Bebb, *1940: Gleanings from a Diary* (*Llyfrau'r Dryw* [Wren Books], 1941), p. 35.
25. John Tyree Fain & Thomas Daniel Young, eds., *The Literary Correspondence of Donald Davidson and Allen Tate* (University of Georgia Press, 1974), p. 230.
26. *Tennessee Historical Quarterly*, *op. cit.*, p. 267.
27. Louis D. Rubin, Jr., ed., "The South: Distance and Change. A Conversation with Robert Penn Warren, William Styron, and Louis

[27] D. Rubin, Jr." *The American South: Portrait of a Culture* (Louisiana State University Press, 1980), p. 311.

[28] George Core, "The Dominion of the Fugitives and the Agrarians," *The American South: Portrait of a Culture, op. cit.*, p. 296.

[29] Thomas A. Underwood, *Allen Tate: Orphan of the South* (Princeton University Press, 2000), p. 156.

[30] C. Vann Woodward, *The Burden of Southern History* (Louisiana State University Press, 1982), p. 32.

[31] Isaiah Berlin, "The Bent Twig: On the Rise of Nationalism," *The Crooked Timber of Humanity: Chapters in the History of Ideas* (John Murray, 1900), p. 246. (Cited in Walter Russell Mead, *God and Gold: Britain, America, and the Making of the Modern World* (Alfred A. Knopf, 2007), pp. 376-7.

[32] Chapman, *op. cit.*, p. 128.

[33] D. Hywel Davies, *The Welsh Nationalist Party 1925-1945: A Call to Nationhood.* (St. Martin's Press, 1983), p. 115.

[34] *1940: Gleanings from a diary, op. cit.*, p. 14.

[35] *Dydd-Lyfr Pythefnos, op. cit.*, p. 65.

[36] David Jones, "Art in Relation to War," *The Dying Gaul and Other Writings* (Faber and Faber, 1978), p. 130.

[37] Plato, "Meno," *The Collected Dialogues of Plato* [Edith Hamilton & Huntington Cairns, eds.] (Princeton University Press, 1996), p. 377.

[38] Core, *op. cit.*, p. 298.

[39] Leader/Op-ed, *Daily Telegraph* (London, 14 April 2008).

[40] Simon Heffer, *Nor Shall My Sword: The Reinvention of England*, (Weidenfeld & Nicolson, 1999), p. 17.

[41] *Ibid.*, p. 92.

[42] *Ibid.*, p. 133.

[43] Berlin, *op. cit.*, p 251.

[44] Mead, *op. cit.*, p. 333.

[45] Johann Gottfried von Herder, *Philosophical Writings* (Cambridge University Press, 2002), pp. 50-1.

[46] Mead, *op. cit.*, p. 333.

[47] Williams, *op. cit.*, p. 39.

[48] Reinhold Niebuhr, *Moral Man and Immoral Society: A Study in Ethics and Politics* (Charles Scribner's Sons, 1932), pp. xxiii-iv.

[49] J.W. Davies, *op. cit.*, p. 78.

[50] R.S. Thomas, "Unity," *Cymru or Wales?* (1992), p. 6; cited in J.W. Davies, *op. cit.*, p. 90.

[51] R. S. Thomas, *Pe Medrwn yr Iaith* [*If I Were Proficient in the Language*] (1988), p. 156; cited in J.W. Davies, *op. cit.*, p. 100.

[52] Jean Delisle, ed., "The Transmission of Cultural Values," *Translators through History* (John Benjamins Publishing Co., 1995), p. 223.

[53] *Ibid.*

[54] Thomas Kinsella, quoted by Garrison Keillor in *The Writer's Almanac* radio broadcast for 4 May 2008 (http://writersalmanac.publicradio.org/).

[55] J.E. Daniel, *Yr Argyfwng* [*The Crisis*], *op. cit.*, p. 7.

Acknowledgments

"Your interest in my father," Mr. Ifan Bebb has written me, "was an unexpected bonus in 2007." But in fact the entire burden of thanks is mine. I must, therefore, express my gratitude first and foremost to this Mr. Bebb. And yet I also feel that no less recognition is due his six siblings, both living and dead, if only because their father appears to have doted so liberally upon them all: Lowri Bebb Williams, Pembrokeshire; Hywel Bebb, Bangor; Sioned Bebb, Bangor; Mererid Bebb Morris (Hywel's twin), deceased; Dewi Bebb, deceased; Owain Bebb, deceased.

I am grateful, as well, to Mr. Christopher Davies of Christopher Davies Publishers, Ltd. for permission to re-issue Bebb's diaries in translation, while fully acknowledging the prior copyrights of the original Welsh works.

Moreover, there are a number of other debts I owe for this book that I can only despair of repaying in full: Tam Le Bailly, in Hay-on-Wye, Powys, Wales, by means of a late-night comment she will never remember, actually inspired in me the willpower and confidence to embark upon my long-term Bebb Project. Her partner, Viv Phillips, along with Steve and Eugenia Winwood and Jay and Stephanie Gore, have provided the companionship and hospitality that have made repeated visits to Wales a glorious addiction for the last 20 years. Meg Sherrill and her colleagues in the Interlibrary Loan Department of the Nashville Public Library, as well as the staff of the Jean and Alexander Heard Library at Vanderbilt University have, on many crucial occasions, streamlined a pothole-strewn path of research. For the cover illustration and design along with the accompanying maps, I have my good friend and frequent co-conspirator Mark Trew to thank. Initially rather vague about his own distant Welsh roots ("somewhere around Pontypridd, I think"), by now his newly restored *Cymreictod* seems to fit like a new pair of trews.

Michael Kreyling, Pete Szilagyi and Vernon Taylor took the trouble to read portions of the work, in-progress; to each of these friends I am beholden for their recommendations and encouragement. I must also thank Rhidian Griffiths for introducing me to Mr. Bebb's family and former publishers; thanks too to Elizabeth Belcher and the Team Tigris book designers at AuthorHouse.

I am grateful to my parents Kermit C. Stengel, Jr., and Suzanne Lafond for imparting to me a congenital, lifelong, unabashed curiosity. And my wife, Terry – who in the company of my three daughters Mary Elizabeth, Morgan Elen and Sara Sudekum, managed the trick of pursing her lips while rolling her eyes at the thought of so many husband-hours spent poring over obscure Welsh texts – deserves a gratitude only the heart can express. *Iti, Cariad, mae'r llyfr hwn wedi ei gyflwyno.*

Regarding endnotes

The few endnotes provided by the author are identified by the inclusion of his name, *W.A. Bebb*. All other notes have been added by the translator.

Recommendations for the pronunciation of Welsh

This is no place, of course, to perfect a Welsh pronunciation out of English-speaking lips and tongues and cheeks. What follow, however, are some of the essential "equivalencies" meant to satisfy the curiosity of the discreet and to spare the embarrassment of the bold.

- AU = "AYE" (close enough for cocktail talk)
- C = "K," always
- CH = gutteral, Germanic "CH," as in "ACH"
- DD = soft "TH," as in "THEM"
- F = "V," always; although a final "F" is often clipped or dropped outright
- FF = an English "F" or "PH"

G = hard "G," always

LL = indescribable, so simply follow Shakespeare's lead and pronounce "FLUELLEN" (or better yet "THLUELLEN") for "LLYWELYN"

TH = hard "TH," as in "THEME"

U = "EE," or the short "I" in "IT"

W = long "OO," as in "SHOOT"

Y = short "I" in some instances (e.g., *wyneb* [face]); and "UH" in others (e.g., *cyfarfod* [meeting])

In virtually every instance, the stress accent in Welsh is on the penultimate (i.e., last-but-one) syllable: *rhagyMA'drodd* [introduction]; *llithRIG'rwydd* [slipperness]; *E'bol* [colt]

The Faraway Paradise

by
W. Ambrose Bebb
M.A. Lecturer/Reader in the Normal College, Bangor, Wales

translated by
Marc K. Stengel
2008

originally published by
Wren Books
Llandebie, Carmarthenshire, Wales
October 1941

About the Book

[original publisher's note from the first (Welsh) edition]

Professor Ambrose Bebb is the author of *1940* [which comprises the second half of the present work]. It is "the most lively, elegant and readable book Wales has seen in quite some time." This particularly interesting volume, on the other hand, is the diary of a Welshman for the year 1841. There's nothing exactly like it to be found written in Welsh, French or English. Indeed, *The Faraway Paradise* will stand as an important contribution to the history and literature of Wales primarily because of the manner in which its author has succeeded in writing a history of his country in a novel, uncomplicated and interesting way that neither distorts nor oversimplifies.

Author's Dedication

For little "Dai," who was ill in hospital when I wrote this small book to ease my pain and longing.

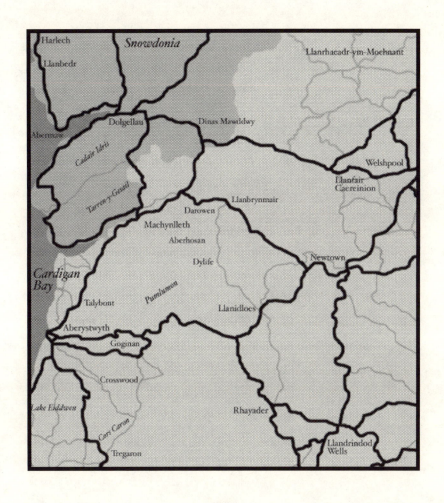

Map for The Faraway Paradise

Preface

I.

It may well be that this short book is a rather presumptuous and over-ambitious attempt to write history in a novel way. It concerns a single, specific year which isn't particularly significant in its own right except for the fact that it took place approximately one century before our own time. The advantage in this approach is that it piques one's curiosity right from the start and encourages a reader to compare the life of a Welshman today with that of a fellow countryman 100 years ago.

After the selection of a specific year, the next step was to select a specific individual who, likewise, bears no special distinctions. It was important to choose an individual who was neither famous nor otherwise remarkable, thereby rendering him more compliant in the hands of his diarist-biographer. It wouldn't pay, for example, to subject the likes of Gwallter Mechain[1] or Tomas Price (Carnhuanawc)[2]; John Elias[3] or John Jones Talysarn[4]; Gwilym Hiraethog[5] or S.R.[6] to as modest an examination as the one proposed for the subject of this diary. It would, moreover, be an advantage should he live somewhere near the middle of Wales, where he would be well placed to catch wind of news from the Gwynedd region in the north and from the area known as Deheubarth in the south, even while he stayed put in his own little Welsh paradise named Powys. As important as any other consideration was a desire that he have a greater range of interests than merely a preoccupation with his religious denomination and its dogmatic concerns.

I am fully convinced that I have come across a man who fulfills virtually all of these qualifications – a man, moreover, upon whom I have a certain claim. He was the brother of my great-grandfather Edward Bebb, and he was someone I know a little bit about and have a certain interest in. We hear a lot about him in the parish of Darowen [7 mi. east of Machynlleth, Montgomeryshire], where people still remember him in spite the fact that he disappeared nearly 100 years ago – in 1847. Thanks to his brother Edward's grandchildren, I learned more about him yet, particularly from a book of "family rules" that he printed up. In addition, there are several surviving letters in his own hand as well as others that he received and turned over to Edward for safekeeping. I am indeed truly indebted to these grandchildren – an aunt and two uncles of mine; namely, Miss Hughes and Mr. Edward Bebb Hughes of Cilwinllan and Mr. William Bebb Hughes of Llwyngronfa – for all of the local lore and personal background information I happen to have.

I only hope they can forgive me for being so bold as to employ this unusual literary device, which I believe has resulted in the only diary-biography of its kind in Welsh, French or English. This book's sole purpose is to persuade the average Welshman to take more of an interest in the history of his homeland. It's simply another way of relating that history without distorting it or minimizing it through oversimplification.

II.

"I, William Bebb, have lived for 30 years on a farm by the name of Rhiwgriafol[7] within Darowen parish, Montgomeryshire. I occupy, therefore, a very central location between North and South Wales. My property is also quite elevated, and my home is surrounded by countryside as hilly as any found in Wales. Rhiwgriafol house stands some 800 feet above sea-level, and it's the highest residence in the entire parish. The land attached to it is remarkably exposed and unsheltered; but because some clever fellow once took care to plant a wood round the house, it is quieter and better protected than many places much lower down. When I step away from this sheltering copse, there is nothing else upon the entire property, except the occasional stone wall, that provides any sort of protection whatsoever. My home, then, is a sort of observation post from which I can gaze down upon all the other farms of the neighborhood – sometimes in great envy.

"But there are advantages to such a lofty altitude as well. Just outside the doorway of my hillside home, one of he most glorious and spectacular views that the eye of man has ever beheld spreads out before me. On a completely clear day, I can see all the way to the summit of Taren y Gesail; all the way to the saddle of Cader Idris; and to the very end of Aran Fawddwy. I gaze out over all of it as my view sweeps in a half-circle from the sea to the shore and then onward behind me towards the foothills of Pumlumon Fach and Pumlumon Fawr. Within this all-encompassing countryside, both far and near, there are hills and uplands, scarps and slopes rising and falling across each others' flanks and shoulders, then descending at times down steep, scarred defiles. There's not a flat patch of land anywhere to be found. Every field one encounters climbs up then down into the laps of these hills and slopes; and it is only on account of the untiring vigilance of the stone walls that the fields themselves don't spirit away with the enveloping mists scudding through these districts daily.

"The grand vista that I view at a distance mirrors almost precisely the situation of my own farm. My terrain is also very uneven and sloping, with an occasional descent into a steep ravine or a narrow, wooded vale. The highest part of the farm rises along a smooth and rather easy grade to the summit of Moelfre, which is about 1,500 feet above sea-level. A good bit of the flatter terrain extends into boggy and rush-filled moors. By the sweat of our brows and dint of our marrowbones, we do manage to coax a bit of produce out of this landscape's tough old hide. As far as the inhabitants of the valleys and dales are concerned, this place is nothing but an exposed, windy wasteland. Yet to me, all it needs is a little tender loving care. Here, in other words, is my opportunity to impose some discipline upon an untamed stretch of land.

"At times, I have to turn my back on Rhiwgriafol when other business calls. On such occasions, I'm always heading downhill – to Melinbyrhedyn and Darowen on Sundays and prayer nights and for *seiat* [fellowship society] meetings; to Llanbrynmair on family errands; to Trefnewydd [Newtown] for the tons of lime I use to slake my farm's meager soil; to Llanidloes, Llanwyddelan and Llanfair Talhaearn for my *Cwrdd Misol* [Monthly Chapel Meetings], Temperance Meetings and *Cymdeithasfa* [Presbyterian Association Meetings]. Some of these outings are quite taxing: It's a good hour's walk to Llanbrynmair, for example; it's seven miles to Machynlleth, about 20 to Llanidloes, and four more yet to Trefnewydd.

"I was born at Tawelan farm, near *Y Bont* [Bont Dolgadfan] outside Llanbrynmair in 1787. I had four brothers, although only one has survived beyond childhood – Edward, that is, who now lives at Cilwinllan farm, which borders mine. I received a bit more than the usual education – attending, first, the school of Rev. John Roberts in The Old Chapel. Then for a term or two, I attended school at Shrewsbury. Afterwards, I came back home to work on the farm – cosy, old Tawelan. But I didn't give up reading or writing. I studied the art of writing letters to every sort of person; and I learned how to draw up a will; how to outfox an attorney intent on gaining an unfair advantage; and how to survey land properly. In particular, I read my Bible and every book on Theology that came my way. I became a deacon in the Methodist chapel of Bont immediately upon reaching my twentieth year.

"Since I was born in Llanbrynmair, it was totally impossible for me not to run into Independent-Congregationalists day after day. As I was just saying, their Minister had been my first teacher. And quite remarkably, another Minister of that denomination was raised at the same hearth as Edward and myself. The Rev. John Breese, of Carmarthen, is the illegitimate son of my mother's brother; and my mother raised him as tenderly as she did Edward and me. After he had grown up, he decided to become a weaver; and he left us for Cwmcarnedd, on the other side of Llanbrynmair. He was now just a step or two away from The Old Chapel, so naturally he became a member there. Before long, he felt compelled to begin preaching. By now, he is regarded as a genuine credit to his denomination, and he is one of the best preachers they have. He is two years younger than I am, and we remain great friends.

"My mother is still alive, and she is remarkably active for a 79-year-old. Currently, she lives with me and at other times with my brother; she alternates between Cilwinllan and Rhiwgriafol as she pleases. She is a woman of authentic religious temperament, and she must have transferred that same temperament to me. On the other hand, there was no hint of such an inclination where my father was concerned. He died 15 years ago, and he refused to become religious even towards the very end. But even though his nature was as different from my mother's as it could possibly be, never was a man more faithful to his wife than he was. Shooting and hunting were his great passions, and this is the agreement he and Mother once reached:

"'Lwlen, if you'll see to it that we men-at-hounds keep our bellies full, you can have all the preachers you want over to the house as often as you please.'

"'Splendid,' she said.

"And those two honored that arrangement for as long as my father lived.

"Well, there you have a little summary of my story for the last 50 years or so – from the end of 1787 until the beginning of 1841. As for my fate during 1841, you'll find an account of that in the Diary which follows."

III.

In an article titled "Land of the Setting Sun," which appeared in the March 1907 issue of *Traethodydd* [*The Essayist*], the late Evan Jones of Caernarfon[8] had occasion to refer to the aforementioned William Bebb, and this is what he said:

"William Bebb was a remarkable man. He was without a doubt one of those few who had received 'the five talents.'[9] He was a prosperous farmer, a good surveyor, an enlightened theologian and a skilled musician."

W. Ambrose Bebb
The Longest Day [21 June], 1941

The Faraway Paradise

A Welshman's Diary from 1841

JANUARY THE 1ST: A new year begins once again – the 41st year of this century, and more or less the 41st in a series of awful years in a hard world. On occasion, one year is slightly better than the rest, of course; but on the whole, times have been quite poor, both during and after the Wars of Napoleon. We were looking forward to the *"Rifform Bil"* ["Reform Bill"],[10] hoping that it would work many miracles. But it did nothing of the sort. Disappointment has followed disappointment right up to today.

There are a lot of uprisings, both great and small, taking place all over the country; and there are more complaints than ever about poverty. It's said that "the poor will always be with us." Well, they are with us; there have never been quite so many of them, in fact.

Several souls have fled to *'Merica*, even from this quiet, rural district. And that includes several of our friends and relatives. They're writing back and urging us to follow. For years, the idea's been on my mind. It's hard to know what's best – terribly hard.

January the 2ⁿᴰ: Ice and snow. My brother Edward shows me a letter he received a while back from Richard Hughes, formerly of Melinbyrhedyn, who is the brother of Edward's wife. Richard went to *'Merica* a few years ago, and now he lives in Ebensburgh[11] at the edge of the Allegheny Mountains in West Pennsylvania. I'll copy part of his long letter – it was written 26 October 1840:[12]

> *"It's a high place, healthy in the summer*, he said about the area, *"and none too hot; and the winters aren't unnaturally cold…and the water is wholesome, with plenty of it…The land is more productive than any back home – in the six parishes of Cyfeiliog,*[13] *that is. As for Ebensburgh, it's small, even though it's a shire town* [a county seat]. *There's no market in it…but we can buy butter in the shops…as well as cheese and meat. All about the place are drovers and herdsmen buying cattle and sheep.*
>
> *"As for giving advice, I can't – since the occasional person who has had a good life back home* [in Wales] *soon finds himself unhappy here. But for everyone else who has had difficulty paying rent and taxes over there, and all those who have despaired of their livelihoods and those of their children, it's unlikely they would feel greatly troubled about having come to America. Because this is a country that's full of goodwill, and I don't know of any diligent, hard-working man who has failed to make a decent life for himself in this place…*
>
> *"I would be pleased to see you here, and I'm confident you would never regret coming. I say this since I believe I'd rather begin a life here without a penny to my name than own a good, well-stocked farm over there. But a lean year over here is a bit worse than it appears because money is so scarce on account of America having paid off a substantial portion of its debt to England. Still, we're expecting better times soon, better than anyone has ever seen. Time will tell. But there's no need to complain too much. There is plenty of goodwill to keep us going…*

> "*As concerns the children, it would be better for them by far to be in America. I have no fear that any of them should ever reproach me for persuading them to come over.*
>
> "*Regarding my sister-in-law's question about what sort of clothes are in fashion here, I think that a person of her age can leave fashion behind and dress herself in proper clothes without any need for a certain hat or cloak or bedgown. Then she'll discover how self-confident and unembarrassed she feels in this country.*
>
> "*As for religion, there are five denominations here – namely, the Independent-Congregationalists, the Anabaptists, the Campbellites,*[14] *the Papists*[15] *and the Methodist Calvinists.*[16] *Many, many Papists… but only 28 Methodists. It so happens that there were 10 of us in the beginning, as of a year ago last May. The Methodists suffer for lack of a preacher, and we'd like William Bebb, Rhiwgriafol, to find us one. In hopes that he might, we beg you to pray for us and do something about it. The cause of the Lord is the same in every land. Be on the lookout, dear brother in Wales. We are starting off virtually unarmed – that is, we've few books suitable for Sunday School. It would be good if you had a chance to send us some, namely six Catechisms and six Confessions of Faith.*
>
> "*I'm expecting to see you over here. You could live with us while you look for a suitable place of your own. Best regards to you, and to Wm. Bebb and his wife and the children…*
>
> "*There are a lot of ardent abstainers* [Temperance-men] *here.*
>
> "*Yours,*
>
> "*Richard and Annah Hughes.*"

How interesting, and how very kind. Still, "the grass is always greener on the other side of the fence."[17] For now, though, I must stay right here where I am.

JANUARY 4TH: The Chartists[18] are agitating again. For some time now, they've been rallying for the purpose of petitioning the Queen to free the "Welsh Martyrs" – Frost, Jones and Williams.[19] One meeting was held on Christmas Day, and the principal speakers were the sons of Frost and Williams. There they were – two lads pleading on behalf of their fathers who had been banished to Tasmania. Could anything have been more likely to play upon the sentiments of tender-hearted Welshmen?

They also met on New Year's Day, at Newport, Gwent. I'm sure many attended, since there was considerable sympathy in the area for the banished fathers who'd been dragged from their homes and torn away from their families. And everyone rallied, I suppose, to denounce the naked oppression of it all. I'm in full sympathy with these folk, even though my denomination, John Elias[20] especially, is opposed to them – opposed to their use of force. Is the use of force un-Scriptural? Who knows? But how forceful can the voice of the poor possibly be without force?

JANUARY 6TH: A bit about that Chartist meeting in Newport. A little over a year ago, a great riot broke out there. But this time, things were rather quieter, although the docks stood idle and hundreds were cast out of work – without any wages in the middle of a cold winter. Why so docile this time, then? Well, the bosses probably feared they'd killed the oxen,[21] so they invited the workers to a New Year's feast. Clever, eh?

Even so, about 2,000 people attended the meeting, pouring in from Nant-y-Glo, Tredegar and Blackwood – the exiles' home towns. One of these Chartists has been up here in Llanidloes, making threats and demanding the return of the exiles. "Demanding their return" – and just how do they suppose they're going to do that? With bare hands against full arms? It'll be dashed hopes yet again. To say nothing about alienating the sympathies of many fine men. Consider this, for example: The Welsh Language Society of London is now offering a prize of two guineas[22] for the best essay upon the topic, "The Harmful

Tendency of Chartism in Wales." What a hot competition that should be!

JANUARY 7TH: Assembly meeting at Abergele Church today. John Jones, of Talsarn, is preaching there twice – John Jones himself with that broad forehead of his, and his fiery eyes, and all the dignity of his person. I'd give a lot to be able to go and see him. … Ffowc Ifans, from Machynlleth, will be there too – so I suppose I'll get the whole story from him then.

Remarkably, John Elias doesn't come. It's hard to know why, unless he's feeling poorly. And yet he's said to be feeling quite well lately, as I understand from reading an account of the great rally he led on Christmas Day for members of the Temperance Society of Llangefni. All told, some 250 of them paraded through town, from the Chapel to the school – with John Elias himself leading the group. They took tea afterwards, and the boys and girls sang songs about "Abstaining from intoxicating drink." Fair enough – but tea? It's not so harmful for the girls, I suppose…but what about John Elias! You won't find tea in our house, that's for sure – except for what Mother takes, that is; and what the wife takes too, when she's ailing.

JANUARY 12TH: I hear Lord Mostyn of Talacre has contributed during the holidays and for New Year's a lot of meats, flannels and blankets to 200 poor families in and around the parishes of Llanasa. A fine thing it is, and very kind of him. It's the same every year. God is generous to him.

Also, Sir Watcyn Wyn's managers, upon receipt of half their rents, are refunding the rent increases. That's good news. But why raise rents at all in such dismal times? Thanks for the gesture, just the same. It's a pity more of our landlords don't follow suit.

I pay £80 in rent for Rhiwgriafol[23] – in other words £10 more than my father paid. My brother, Edward, pays £56 for Cilwinllan, which is more than the previous tenant paid when the farm had more fields than Edward has now. Still, I always manage to pay in-full, even though I don't make much of a profit.

20 January: I'm on an errand to Machynlleth today, and I've put the boys to work – they're threshing again. It's hard work, and it takes almost all winter to finish. There aren't any threshing machines in our shire, or anywhere else for that matter until you get over towards Denbighshire. They're far too expensive.

In town, there's a lot of talk about market fairs; there are some pretty good prices over towards Aberystwyth and Llanbedr. Things seem to be better than they have been for a long time; cows-in-calf are selling fairly high. And there's a good bit of hawking and haggling over horses and sheep, and for fattened cattle and hogs. On the whole, a pretty good showing lately.

I run into Ffowc Ifans. He can't say enough about that Church Assembly meeting. John Jones of Talsarn was just so full of that "immortal passion." And he tells me John Elias is complaining about his foot – is worried he may have gangrene. If so, he can keep it!

Ffowc also reports that the old bard, Dewi Wyn of Eifion[24] died last Sunday morning – due to a long illness and sunken spirits. I wasn't too familiar with his work, nor did I understand much of what little I came across.

Once again, I encounter the occasional drunkard hanging about – in Maengwyn Street, to say nothing of The Garrison[25] – despite all our preaching against drink. Shame on us, as a denomination. And I have it on good authority that the Welsh Language Society of Swansea is offering a prize of 42 shillings[26] for the best lines devoted to the topic, "*On Temperance.*"

24 January: *Anti-loving-in-the-bed!* That's the name of a newly established Society in Dolgellau, according to a letter we received from my wife's family.[27] What a delightfully amusing name, but an excellent idea even so – as are the various other Purity Leagues that have recently been founded. There ought to be one in every district. People call this sort of immorality "a national custom"[28]; but it's a hobgoblin of ours from Anglesey to Cardigan. John Elias has railed against it like a valiant field marshal. But it persists nonetheless – even amongst us here in Montgomeryshire. In our district, I'll fight it to the bitter end. You see, I have a set of "rules" – for heads of families – that's almost ready for distribution.

29 January: Friday. On Tuesday, Parliament was opened by the Queen. All pomp and pageantry, of course. I read her address, very carefully. What a peculiar speech – like a bladder full of wind. Is there a single word about Chartism? Not one! Or about the distress of plain folk throughout the countryside? Why, yes, there's this small crumb: "*The authority of the Deputies appointed to reform the Poor Laws terminates at the end of this year. I am relying on you to give serious attention to those matters bearing so intimately upon the general welfare of the public.*"

Words, words! That's all we get. Meanwhile the poor are starving and dying from sheer lack of *bread*. Despite the fact that this accursed law, the New Poor Act, has been imposing its dead hand upon their lives – rather, upon their dying agonies – for seven years now. Our unfortunates are being cast upon the mercies of the *un*merciful poor houses, and old men and women are being separated from one another after living together for years. Once, the vow of marriage declared, "Until death do us part"; today it decrees, "To the *wyrcws*" [workhouse]![29]

But what does that little lass over there on her throne know about anything?[30] Even more importantly, what do *they* – all those

"Milords and gentlemen" of Parliament – know? What's the difference between them and their confounded parties? Whigs? Sure: we expect bread from them. But what we get instead – those snakes! – are laws with the barbs of a scourge fastened to them!

30 JANUARY: Saturday. Edward, my brother, calls by from Cilwinllan to fetch Mother, who will stay with him for the next few weeks. She alternates between staying with him and with me these days. And she says that a person can get by with a scrap of clothing less over there as compared with here [since Rhiwgriafol is so windy and exposed]. Edward shows me another letter from *'Merica*, from the same Richard Hughes as before. It's dated 18 December 1840, from Ebensburgh. It's as long as the previous one, but it rambles a bit more. Richard's thankful for the letter he received, "*last spring, and for the stockings you sent to Richard Tudor...I realized that I needed to send a letter answering your questions in as much detail as I can provide.*" He would have answered sooner, he said, "*except that I had quite a lot to learn on your behalf*"!

So here's more "*of the story from 'the new country'*:

"*For poor folk, it's far superior here to Britain. It was miserable to see by your letter that the poor are suffering such distress in Wales, whose virtues are so abundant. Without a doubt, there's not the first whisper nor sigh to be heard from the poor about any sort of oppression hereabouts, nor is there such talk about putting up any sort of* Pwar hows *[Poor house] for anyone. There's enough work for everybody and good wages for doing it. There's enough food for man and beast at reasonable prices. There's plenty of wheat to be had for under a dollar a bushel – that's eight gallons, mind – and everything else is comparably priced.*

"*But even though I and many others consider America far superior to Wales, there are numerous others here who are quite unhappy for sundry reasons – especially men like yourselves who hadn't much suffered any particular Distress in their own affairs back in Wales. Several of these sort do complain for a while about some of the unpleasant things they encounter. But I can inform you that this year, I didn't see much increase in that scarcity of money that I mentioned previously, even though goods themselves are cheaper. For nearly four years, the money situation over here hasn't been particularly good…because America has paid off a lot of debt… with hard currency, especially…*

"*One of the Whigs will begin to rule the United States on the next 4th of March, and he's a descendent of Gomer, they say* [31] *— someone by the name of [Benjamin] Harrison. But, my dear brothers and sisters, my thinking is, if you're at all undecided about coming to America, I'd recommend that you come at the first opportunity. Because it's a good time to buy land just now; and there won't be any great pressure to sell for quite some time. But if you do decide to come, let me know as soon as possible…and after you reach the Head of the Alleghenies, within nine miles of Ebensburgh, I'll bring a wagon to fetch you…And if you could bring a dozen copies of the Confession of Faith and a half-dozen of…*(this part is torn away)*… by Mr. Charles of Bala.* (From here on, one half of the sheet is missing…) On the back, there's this: "*David Lewis wishes to send his most affectionate regards to W. Bebb of Rhiwgriafol and to his family.*

"*…get to see y–*
Face to face
thinking of you in Wal–
Richard and Annah

1ST OF FEBRUARY: Monday, and another work-week begins. The boys are putting the horses and cattle out to graze and making a go of the threshing. I am too; and I'm also walking the fields and the mountain pasture whose stone enclosure I've almost finished building.

Back to the house at nightfall; I read the paper by the light of a rush candle. A story about the burial of the old bard Dewi Wyn…from over a week ago. Not particularly "bearable" for everyone concerned.

The body was borne[32] by his fellow tenants and next-door neighbors. Several ministers rode out ahead of the body…several more behind. And here we have the Welsh Language Society of London offering a silver medallion worth three guineas as a prize for the six best *englyn* verses composed as an epitaph for the bard. How true indeed is that old saying: "If it's fame you want, you have to die first."

At suppertime, everyone's around the great table – we have porridge with milk and oat bread. Then it's various domestic chores and off to bed before ten.

FEBRUARY 6TH: An eclipse of the moon tonight. The entire sky appears brooding and still. We all turn out of the house to watch in wonder and awe. As the saying goes, "Enlightment dawns night by night."[33] Over yonder, the rocks of Cader Idris rear up all swarthy in the dusk.

Back to our fire and rush candles. While the wife and the girls finish the housework, the field hands and my two sons fashion wooden spoons, baskets, threshing flails and *prennau rhaffau* [wooden implements for making hay-ropes]. And the village tailor entertains us from his seat at the head of the table. So much for *his* lack of children!

FEBRUARY THE 7TH: Sunday. Wind and rain, at their very worst. No matter, I'm off to Chapel anyway with the majority of the family joining me. We're soaking wet after passing through the moor along the *wtra*.[34] It's only a mediocre sermon, and the old, small chapel is mostly empty. Over to my brother Edward's for dinner. Mother's doing fine. The houses and the outbuildings are deep in shadow. After dinner, I'm off again to Llan Darowen for the afternoon service. Home later for bowls of flummery[35] and back to Melinbyrhedyn in the evening. I scold a tippler or two along the way, then home again – wet to my skin. Reading, praying – then to bed, completely worn out.

FEBRUARY THE 8TH: What a rascal this harsh weather is. An uncommonly cold wind is scouring the entire countryside. The wooded slope that surrounds the house is heaving in great sobs; and the house itself shakes to its foundation. Several houses of the village have lost either their roof or a window. Both man and beast are struggling; and the wretched sheep bleat pitifully from morning 'til night. They seek shelter amongst one another, nearly piling up on each other's backs. They're hunkered together next to the hedgerows and stone walls. Thank goodness for those hedgerows and stone walls. It's as if Cader Idris and Aran Mawddwy were themselves trembling against the gale. To the house!

FEBRUARY 10TH: The winds persist, and so does the devastation of the woods and the houses. More news: in the quarry districts, everyone is sheltering in their homes; no one works. Two thousand workers at Dinorwic, in Caernarfonshire, haven't been able to accomplish anything for days. From throughout the entire country comes news about winter hardship and its effects upon the poor. Many are dying solely from lack of food. I ponder deeply that old saw, "Blessed are the lives of the poor"![36] What's so blessed about them?

FEBRUARY 12: With the end of the gale a looming silence spreads. Then a great, drenching rain. The boys are cleaning out the pig sties and calf pens. I myself walk the fields. I read the paper after dinner. One story concerns a few temperance meetings here and there. It's a major preoccupation of our time – for the last four or five years now, in fact. It's seven years since old John Roberts of Llanbrynmair died. He kept beer in the house all the time, and his wife brewed it. As at *Y Diosg*[37] so too at every other farmhouse. Eventually, almost every cottage and bothy throughout the land has become a tavern, and men get drunk before going to work in the morning! That accursed *Beer Act* of 1830 has made it possible for everyone who so desires to keep a tavern. Drinking and getting drunk have become a plague. It's high time we had a *Temperance Movement*; and I give my everlasting thanks for it. I myself have given up brewing beer and formed a *Temperance Society* in Melinbyrhedyn – one in Abercegir, too. And a "Society Against Tobacco" as well.[38] No beer in the Chapel House is how it will be from now on; and no beer for the preacher either, before his sermon or after – even though several of them are still plenty thirsty for it!

The Movement is succeeding in spite of all. Take that publican over in Newborough, in Anglesey – he was censured, and his pub shingle[39] was pulled from his house and nailed to the door of his pigsty. Way to go!

It's all to do with John Elias' influence, that's for sure.

13 FEBRUARY: Llanidloes Fair today. I go – not so much for the fair but to see Williams the Printer. I want him to print my "Rules" for religious families. I have nine rules, each one dedicated to maintaining religion and godliness at the hearthsides of our homes in these precincts. Later, I'll be giving them to all the chapels round here.

I promise to keep them short and simple.

I run into a couple of fellows here and there, and we talk about what's going on in the world. Such complaining there is. The weavers have been the backbone of community life in Llanidloes for generations. But now, their circumstances are miserable – nearly 800 of them face lack of work, and they're just wasting away unpaid. What will come of it all, I simply can't say. Is it any wonder that they should have mutinied last year?

Glimpses of Life in Wales

I call in at Wmffre [Humphrey] Gwalchmai's and buy a copy of *Athraw* [*The Tutor*]. Read it at home – a very good issue. There's an article by John Elias in it on "The Importance of Ministry." He says there aren't any other callings in the world that can compare with this one. How very true, if only everyone would realize it. But most folks are merely speckled birds[40] – just so many "Jacks," as Brutus[41] calls them.

It was good for my soul to see John Elias' name again. Give him his due! When he's on his own turf – that is to say, in his pulpit – there's no one else can match him.

14 FEBRUARY: *Sunday.* To Chapel, all day. Everybody goes, except for *one* who stays home to prepare dinner. Everybody takes a turn staying home to make dinner on Sunday mornings, be it a farm hand, a drover, whoever.

Sunday School continues to thrive. Supper is soup and meat. Then, everybody turns to his Bible – no other book is so much as opened on Sundays; not *Drysorfa* [*Treasury*], not *Dirwestwr* [*Temperance-man*], not *The Tutor*.

16TH OF FEBRUARY: Tuesday night. I finish reading *The Tutor* – even the long article by Sam Roberts in which he comes out against Lewis Edwards of Bala – that old rascal! He might as well throw in the towel.[42] He's just like a drunk who's been tossed on his backside yet keeps on shouting he'll get even. And I'll tell him so to his face, as soon as I get hold of him. He and his bunch of blather are nothing but a shabby heap from one end to the other: *Mr. Edwards of Bala, President of the Conference, Moderator of the General Assembly, His Reverence of Canterbury, his Holiness of Rome, Arch-Rabbi of the Synagogue, and the Lord High Chancellor.*" The man is going mad with all this foolish and illogical nonsense.

I loathe that old argument between Presbyterians[43] and Independents – I have close relatives who are Methodists, and others who are Independents. And here we are jabbering on about it daily. So far as the Editor of *Haul* [*The Sun*; an Anglican periodical] is concerned, we're only to be taken seriously as the butt of jokes. For shame!

20ᵀᴴ ᴏꜰ Fᴇʙʀᴜᴀʀʏ: I'm gleaning the week's news, and I wind up hollering at the papers over what I read. How about this gem: a so-called *apparition* has manifested in Carmarthen! Hundreds of beings are marching quietly through the streets of the town in the dead of night – and they're all wearing white garments and crying out in unison, "*Nine thousand Welshmen without a welcome in Church on Sabbath eve!*" Every time they pass the New Church of St. David, they strike the gate; and, with a voice from the grave, they shout, "*Welsh! Welsh! Welsh!*" What, in the name of mankind, is *this*? An attempt to awaken the Church of England to its obligations towards the Welsh Language? So it seems to me. Surely, there's justification enough, what with all those English-speaking Bishops – and even in spite of occasional fine Parsons like old Gwallter Mechain of Llanreadr Mochnant and, especially, Thomas Price (Carhuanawc).[44] What if people should get Bishops the likes of these two?

Anyway, a stunning success for the apparition in its holy whites – devout Welsh Chartists, I'll warrant.

Fᴇʙʀᴜᴀʀʏ 23ᴿᴰ: The Welsh Indians are starting to come into view once again. It's said they're the descendants of Prince Madog. I wonder? It's pretty hard to believe, even though quite a few Welshmen in '*Merica* mention them in their letters home – after seeing them and hearing them speak Welsh. These Madogwys Indians say that their ancestors came from across the sea! Several people have even tried to trace the history of these Indians, and one or two have lost their lives in the attempt – the occasional one rather unbalanced in the head, it would seem![45] Now, there's word that some Welsh emigrants to *'Merica* are organizing two troops to proceed up both banks of the Missouri River next spring. A witch's dream,[46] as far as I'm concerned. Our friend Hughes, formerly of Melinbyrhedyn, certainly believes in them; and he thinks we Welsh should distribute Bibles amongst these Indians. A right good idea – if there be any foundation to the story!

FEBRUARY 25TH: Two news items that cancel each other out. One is about Temperance in Ireland – just the thing to encourage us here in Wales.

The other is a piece of tripe – about the growth of Papistry in Wales? The Catholics have just opened a Chapel in Newport [Gwent], and they now number 3,000 – nearly as many as the entire population of Llanidloes. In 1812, there weren't but five of them there. What prodigious growth. It's the Irish, of course – what's more, they live 15 or 20 to a house. Savages. Papists are the Nonconformists' worst enemies in Wales, and I say this even though I once belonged to the faction that favored giving them their freedom back in 1829. Now, in light of this news, if ever there were a better reason for us Nonconformists to leave off our family feuding, I for one can't think of it.

FEBRUARY 27TH: Saturday afternoon, and I'm back into the house to get out of the rain. A bit of prattle with my two youngest daughters, Margiad and Siân, one each on my knees. Reading the paper, I ponder this story for a while: It's about some old man, 81 years old, by the name of William Jones of Llangadfan in Anglesey, who was forced to spend his days in bed just to stay warm. Meantime, his wife was off begging for bread for the both of them. She returned home one day, and there he was on his bed of chaff with nothing over him but one blanket and two hopsacks. He had died! – while *she* was scurrying round trying to scrape up a few crusts of barley bread to take back to the house. An inquiry followed…and it concluded that two shillings a week would have been enough for them to keep body and soul together. Imagine that: no fire in the depth of winter. No bread, not even crumbs! Either begging or lying out on a bed of straw are the only two choices left for thousands of my fellow countrymen. Well, not quite: there's one other alternative, and that's to break in and steal. O! Wales…*if* indeed it *is* you who are responsible.

March 1st: "March kills you, April skins you."[47] But the new month comes in like a little lamb – after all, what could be worse than last month's storm! There's a bit of snow on the ground – "a savvy snowfall suspects a sequel"[48] sure enough. I start working the land again after taking quite a bit of time off. Thanks to the fine weather, I can enclose fields and do some digging. So far this year, threshing grain by hand and putting the horses and cattle out to graze have been the extent of our chores.

The days lengthen, and spring draws near. The lambs start to arrive – five quite small ones are shivering; their mothers are weak and milk-barren. Every day now, their whiteness flecks moor and mountain pasture somewhere or other; and their thin bleats of "me-me" are borne upon the winds. The first, uncertain voices of spring. And many thanks for 'em! Shepherding will be my chief preoccupation for the next two months – and I'll have a bottle of milk with me each time I make my rounds.

March the 2nd: Yesterday was Machynlleth Fair, but I wasn't there. From someone who was I hear that there was a lot of scuttlebutt about a certain letter Frost[49] posted home to his wife.

"What did the wretch have to say?" I ask

"The only smattering I caught was this: Neither he nor Jones nor Williams have suffered any punishment at all."

"No punishment at all, you say? He's been exiled from his family in Tasmania! Surely, that's punishment enough in itself."

The fellow who told me all this was a Tory, and I'll warrant the Tories are beside themselves trying to inflict even more punishments upon these Chartist rogues.

MARCH 5TH: The paper is full of talk about St. David's Day Assemblies – in London, that is – with the Bishops of Bangor and St. David's speaking and the Earl of Powys presiding. Lots of speechifying, great feasting and boasting and carousing – so non-Welsh and, most certainly, so non-Temperance! Such nonsense it all is: just so much wanton foolishness.[50] It's the same again in Liverpool. What a bag of smoke! Heaven forbid they should actually consider *doing* something for Wales, instead of carrying on and getting drunk off of her horn o' plenty.

MARCH 6TH: A great day in Welshpool. Today the judge, Sir John Williams, has arrived before setting out on his circuit-ride through the North. Tomorrow morning, the Sabbath, there will be much merrymaking and great splendor within the church. And Gwallter Mechain will deliver a sermon – that old creature is 80 years old, mind you!

After dinner, I take two mares to be shoed at the smithy in Darowen. The [Anglican] parson happens to cross my path. We speak, and he's amiable enough – even though he's but a shadow on the wall compared to his predecessor, old Tomas Richards. Now *there* was a magnanimous parson for you. "*The Methodist Parson*" is what everyone called him. He'd loan me copies of *The Sun* all the time. So does this parson sometimes – like today, for instance. On the way home, I'm turning the pages of *The Sun*. There's a story about *"The Shepherds of Eppynt."*[51] As usual, it's full of alternating truths and lies. *"The Ungodly are on the advance"* is another headline; and there's a huge article on *"Oddfellowship."* It's a benevolent society, says *The Sun*, and its roots go back to the Garden of Eden. That's telling it like it is! The old patriarchs, the prophets, the evangelists and the apostles were all… Oddfellows. The best lie is the obvious lie,[52] that's for sure! If the Oddfellows are so benevolent, why then all the "mystery" surrounding them, what with this secret lodge over here and that one over there? Why, there's a new "lodge" in Llanidloes and another one in Tregaron. And the same goes for the "Ivorites" and their lodges, even though they're always talking about "nurturing the Welsh language." Why don't they operate openly, in the clear light of day? Is it any wonder why the Presbyterian Association of Denbigh strictly forbids members in its Fellowship to have anything to do with Oddfellows?

MARCH THE 9TH: A copy of *The Treasury* arrives today. My eyes alight upon an article by John Elias on *"Preaching the Gospel."* He lists three headings:

What is 'preaching the Gospel'?

Who preaches it?

What's the point of preaching it?

I read the article slowly, carefully. It's incomparably good. Out in the fields, with the sheep and the lambs, I ponder its implications over and over again. John Elias at his best.

MARCH THE 12TH: Llanbrynmair Fair – the best cattle market in the shire. I take a few good yearlings and see that others are also driving cattle along every mountain path down towards Dolgadfan. The place is full of animals, every step of the way from Dolgadfan to Y Bont at the Wynnstay Estate. There are quite a number of drovers there, and I'm forced to prattle with them in that muck of a language they call English. You'd think, by their occasional grimaces, that our cattle weren't worth beans – although the blacks from Cilwinllan and Dolbacho are as good as ever. It's a dismal situation. I *have* to sell my best ones, for lack of feed; and I turn the others towards home – to corn cribs that will be emptier every day from now on.

I come upon Sam[53] and Risiart Roberts. They're both complaining about the hard times – the drovers turning their noses up at our cattle; butter at six or seven pence a pound; cheese at a pence and a half. Sam's still talking about *'Merica* – he just recently heard from my first-cousin, Wm. Bebb, in Ohio. A very good harvest there this year. "The grass is greener on the other side," I think to myself; but I feel the same way they do. "Emigration" – it's a word on many people's lips. And no wonder, what with the oppression of the *Tithe* and the *Church Tax* and that accursed *New Poor Tax* keeping the common folk down, and even breaking up their homes. Wales – a country abounding in virtues? A country abounding in afflictions is more like it.

MARCH THE 18TH: The boys have almost finished the ploughing. We start sowing. We sow during the day and tend to our shepherding before and after, morning and evening. Over 100 lambs by now – some are feeble, and several have died. Quite a loss.

MARCH THE 21ST: Sunday. Everyone's off to chapel except for our head foreman. It's his turn to make dinner today. Everyone else goes to meeting – the wife and children, farm hands and serving girls, as usual (if there's any such thing as "usual," that is).

A mediocre sermon, by one of those "traveling Jacks," like Brutus himself. A shilling for a sermon like that is more than enough.

It's dinner in Cilwinllan on my way to afternoon service in Llan Darowen. Mother is quite comfortable. I tend to family chores till day's end, then I'm off to bed shortly after nine.

22ND OF MARCH:[54] Very busy yesterday and today – with both the sowing and the shepherding, morning and evening. The days are lengthening, so there's less time to read. I'm only turning pages, really, not reading at all. Just gleaning from between the covers. Today, a book by Robert Ifans, of Llanidloes – *A Chatechism for Temperance*. Very useful for us right now.

27TH OF MARCH: A week of hard work. We finish the sowing; haul barrels of lime from Newtown and spread a lot of it about; climb and run after the sheep. I carry the weak ones to the house – to the barnyard, and the sickly ones are put in care of my wife Margiad. Tonight, Saturday night, there's just enough time to read two pieces in the magazines. One's an article about Brittany, which includes a letter by some Welshman who was there over 15 years ago – a fellow named Dafydd Jones. The Bretons, he says, are closely related to us, but detest the English. For the same reasons we do, I fancy. But they're all Papists, the poor wretches! What a brilliant idea it would be to send over a mission amongst them.

28TH OF MARCH: The Sabbath – a full, heavenly day. Tomas Hughes of Machynlleth preaches remarkably well. His little boy is with him, and the little pup is a very agreeable lad. The two of them are staying at Cilwinllan.

30TH OF MARCH: I'm with the boys, both of them. We walk the countryside and do our shepherding. I count the lambs – 165 of them. Many more have yet to be born. We find Edward, my brother, up on the sheep-walk at Cilwinllan, and he tells us a tale or two about Tomas

Hughes – who still holds quite harsh opinions on the subject of drinking! On Monday morning, he sent his small son down from the loft with a message for Edward's wife. He was to tell her that his father wasn't feeling at all well. And did she go up to see for herself? Indeed, she dropped what she was doing, and asked him directly,

"Well, what's wrong with *you*, Tomas Hughes?"

"I'm very poorly, little Mrs. Bebb…very poorly."

"O! you're poorly, are you? Wouldn't it be better for you to get up and get yourself home as soon as you can?"

"…Might you…do you have…a small drop, perhaps…at the bottom of a bottle?"

"Why, no!…not the one drop. But I do have a drop of pale wormwood[55] you can have…"

"You're a hard woman, Mrs. Bebb…a hard woman!"

And Tomas Hughes promptly rose and had a bellyful to eat before high-tailin' it out of there!

3ʳᴰ ᴏꜰ Aᴘʀɪʟ: I read in the paper that Parliament's discussing reforms to the New Poor Act. More poor houses, likely enough. Why *not* beautify the countryside with their gloomy presence and haughty officials? And herd even more poor folk – after the men and women have been separated, that is – into them to perish. Enough with all this reforming! The best reform of all would be to abolish the Act, every last letter of it. It's cruel and oppressive and a disgrace to our country. Why, it's enough to draw the Judgment of the Almighty down upon us.

8ᵀᴴ ᴏꜰ Aᴘʀɪʟ: There was a horrible calamity at the Iron Works in Dowlais the day before yesterday. Workers were repairing the furnace, and the walls fell in on them. Altogether, eight of them were buried alive. Very sobering, indeed. What sort of place for men is that old iron works?

Yet…lots of small crofters, and good field hands too, are swept up from the backcountry into the abomination of the coal pits and the iron works! The countryside is swiftly being de-populated. All this running off to the works and these emigrations to *'Merica* are drawing off our cream. How terribly disheartening!

12TH OF APRIL: Rejoice, rejoice! The "Rules" I've prepared for heads of families have arrived today. I've had a deuce of a time thinking them up; and now here they are, direct from Williams the Printer, Llanidloes:

[*Father's name here*]: **Rules for his Family**

---

1. Undertake to read, to learn and to contemplate the scriptures: and if unable to read, endeavor to learn to do so. John 5:39.[56]

2. Prepare as a family to worship the Lord, and go to public worship whenever this is possible. Jeremiah 10:25.[57]

3. Do not take the name of the Lord in vain; do not swear or curse, tell untruths or use any defiled expressions. Ephesians 4:29.[58]

4. Do not defile the Sabbath, either by sleeping immoderately, strolling or speaking about things unrelated to the day. – Also, respect every means of achieving grace, such as Sunday School, Prayer Meetings, listening to sermons, etc.; and be willing to accompany the family to worship services, except when it is necessary to stay behind to look after the house. Joshua 24:25.[59] (See the 4th Commandment.[60])

5. Obey those in authority in the family in every lawful thing, and be gracious to every family member. Colossians 3:22.[61]

6. Do not attend any corrupt gatherings, or do anything to support them; this includes beer or shooting parties under the guise of

charity; drunken funeral wakes; *nosweithiau llawen* ["nights of mirth"]; football matches; and suchlike things. Ecclesiastes 11:9.[62]

7. Do not go to fairs, unless there be an errand that cannot be done some other time. When such is the case, one is at liberty to go; but come home early, without having partaken of the debased customs of the fair. Genesis 34:1,2.[63]

8. Do not run off to sleep or to a dark place during the festivities prior to a wedding. Job 24:15,[64] Proverbs 7:7-9.[65] And every consideration with respect to another place and time is promised to him who disports himself decently. Also, if whomever you are associating with cannot get another time, despite asking earnestly and offering to compensate their masters for it, only in this circumstance are you permitted a bit of time off, albeit rarely, when the family is sleeping.[66]

9. Show only faithfulness in all things, as if to the Lord and not to men.

And whoever persists in breaking a rule, let that one leave the family, after getting a proper warning and coming to terms over payment for time served in proportion to the year's wages. Psalm 101:6,7.[67]

I will distribute these rules in this parish and in adjacent districts, in hopes that they will be an instrument both for the promotion of religion and good morals and for defense against depravity.

APRIL THE 15TH : More families from these parts are setting out towards Liverpool – and there boarding ships bound for *'Merica*. It's the same thing almost every year. About half the population has departed.[68]

APRIL THE 28TH: I recall that the *Newtown Church Association* meeting opens today. I'm unable to put the work and cares of the farm behind me. It'll have to be tomorrow! I'll leave here in the afternoon, and I'll be there for tomorrow's evening session, as well as for the meeting of Preachers and Deacons at eight o'clock, Friday morning.

APRIL THE 30TH: In Newtown with its population of 4,000 – three-quarters of whom work in the wool trade with its 50 factories. The whole place is remarkably crowded – preachers, deacons, church members. I run into many people I know, and I talk a spell with John Hughes of Pontrobert and Dafydd Morgan of Welshpool. There's the occasional unfamiliar face: Roger Edwards of Bala, for example – rather young, a pleasant enough appearance, a bit fiery perhaps. John Hughes is as untidy as ever, in both demeanor and dress.

We hear a report concerning "The Cause" in the shire. There's been no great increase in church participation anywhere. Still, the Temperance Cause has given a good accounting of itself. Even so, in virtually every church there are more who aren't Temperance Men than those who are – we in Melinbyrhedyn are well ahead in our support of The Cause.

Some setbacks: three or four preachers of the shire have emigrated to *'Merica* in just these last few weeks.

Worst of all – John Elias is quite unwell, with gangrene of the foot. Everyone is dismally sad on account of the news; and we decide to send him a letter of sympathy, to this effect:

Dear Reverend Brother:

We are obliged to acknowledge gratefully the grace of God that has kept you in the Ministry for nearly half a century. You have attained a prominent place amongst us over this long spell, without soiling your robes or losing your crown.

Our hope and prayer is for the Lord of the harvest to extend your days…so that you may yet toil upon his field. We greatly desire to see you at the June Church Association meeting…and nothing is too difficult for the Lord.

How well we understand, dear brother, that the truths you have preached throughout your lifetime are the stuff of comfort in your own affliction. We have no doubt that the Lord Christ, whom you have served since youth, will not refuse you when your strength fails. Loyal is He who called you, who calls even now. You are receiving this letter as a sign of our warmest affection for you, and of our mindfulness of you in your present state of affliction.

A very dispirited atmosphere, with tears behind everyone's sentiments. May God protect him!

1 MAY: May Day![69] – and yet the weather is so cold, the pastures so scanty, the corn crib so empty. Nevertheless, we will carry on as best we can – if only we could have some warmth alternating with some rain.

Yesterday, while in Llanbrynmair on the road home from Newtown, I saw Edward Hughes of Cwmcarnedd; and even he was complaining, despite being something of a landlord himself. Some of his relatives are in *'Merica* also.

There was talk yesterday about establishing an "Oddfellows Lodge" in Llanbrynmair – and lots of enthusiasm for it, too. The ringleaders[70] of the neighborhood were entertaining all the local men of influence, going from manor to manor inviting the gentry to a great dinner. The Vicar attended, as did Rev. John Roberts (S.R.'s brother), Hughes himself and many others – not to mention the representatives of Oddfellows from other towns. And all of it so openly…!

Thirty members joined, Hughes said – "so we can become more estimable men." What a waste all this nonsense is…"become more estimable men"?

MAY THE 3ʳᴅ: I heard today that the folks who departed this shire some three weeks ago just left Liverpool for the City of New York. There were over 150 of them – from this shire [Montgomeryshire] as well as from Merionethshire.

They're planning to buy about 20 square miles of land, raise houses on it and build a chapel in their midst. They want to call the place *Cymru Newydd* [New Wales]! Best wishes to them, after taking all that trouble. Good luck, too, staying all together in one group instead of drifting apart in that flood of immigrants from various countries, like so many others before them.

But if they can…then might I consider going myself perhaps?

MAY THE 4ᵀᴴ: The weather is brightening a bit.

Two years ago, during these early days of May, there was an awful bit of trouble in Llanidloes. It was dismal! For several days – but less than a week – the town was in the hands of the Chartists. Risiart Jarman, Charles Jones and Thomas Powell were in charge; and strange accounts were circulating out of there by way of Newtown, then Dylife and Aberhosan, to us over here.

Nobody was interested in anything else. If London herself had been on fire, not a soul would have so much as inquired about it. There was no other topic of conversation. Even at Prayer Meeting, the Llanidloes uprising was the focus of our entreaties.

Moreover, the air was full of the strangest rumors: about policemen sent out from London; about the entire town assaulting them before they had scarcely shown their beaks. Then came word of soldiers on their way up from Brecon, over from Chester – from Ireland even. It was said they got the coldest reception ever as they made their way through the countryside and villages.

We next heard about how the soldiers divvied up as they approached, closed in upon the town from opposite sides, and…went in. A dreadful silence followed – for a day or two. Then someone ran up, out of breath, to say that many of the Chartists had fled, under cover of darkness, into the countryside where they hid themselves within hay stacks and thickets of gorse.

The nervous trembling lasted for days, and no one alive will ever forget it. Ultimately, the punishments were handed out: some got "transportation" [to Australia] for 15 years, others for seven; and several got hard time in jail, even two women. I know deep down I don't sympathize with them, since I can't in the least countenance their willingness to take up arms. Then again, what alternative did these pitiful creatures have? Their circumstances were miserable, and none of their betters was willing to raise a finger for their sakes.

MAY THE 9TH: The weather keeps improving. It's fair and warm. Everything's growing as far as the eye can see.

John Elias is frequently in my thoughts…and in my prayers every day. The Lord will restore him! I recall the times William Howel of Celli Dywyll and I would set out together to listen to him at the Session Meeting in Bala every year. How we looked forward to hearing him, and we would recite his sermons out loud to one another.

And that poor William Howel[71] took down every word of the sermons in shorthand. He says he did it for years – for a quarter-century, perhaps?

MAY 22ND: Today, Sir Watkyn comes of age – as all men of Powys do eventually. People are saying that Powys and Gwynedd will burst into a blaze of rejoicing for the occasion; and some even call him "Prince of Wales." Maybe it's true…considering his wealth, at any rate. Moreover, if truth be told, he's a better landlord than the half of them.

May 23rd: Sunday. Everyone's off to chapel for the service — except the one preparing dinner! In the afternoon, I devote myself to The Cause on behalf of the weak in Darowen, and I preach a few words on the subject of *"Religion in our Time"*: Where was there ever so much Bible reading as here? When were there ever so many prayers and prayer meetings as now? When was there ever so much discussion of religion as there is today? The countryside is flowering like paradise, we're told.

Really, I wonder?

What about all the debased traditions that still endure? So much drunkenness around, and even temperance-men are breaking their pledges all the time. And afterwards, smoking…more's the pity. At funerals, you can see men pulling out their pipes as if they were in a public-house. It's an abomination! Then at prayer vigils, you can hear them reading letters from *'Merica*, which leads them to the subject of farming — both over here and over there — followed by discussions of buying and selling at market and so forth. When they should be reading the Holy Scripture.

This is supposed to be a flowering of religion?

Most significantly of all: Where is the righteousness? Where is the kindness? Here we are not doing a thing in the world to alleviate the distress of our poor. Nothing, that is, except to refer them to the local *Board of Guardians*, to herd them into those unspeakable *Wyrcws* [Workhouses] or into one of the mills established by the New Poor Act! This is supposed to be a *flowering*?

May 29th: I see the story of Sir Watkyn's coming-of-age celebration in Welshpool last Saturday. Vanity Fair, all day long. In the morning, a volley of 21 shots – just in case the town's inhabitants had somehow forgotten. In the afternoon, a peal of bells from St. Mary's Church; and the thundering of a tabard-drum throughout the day. And then, the most remarkable games: Racing to snatch a hat off the top of a high pole. Donkey and pig and barrow races. Vying to be the longest-enduring smoker! And drunkenness – even amongst the temperance-men! Dinner for the children of the Free School; and another dinner for the gentry at the *Royal Oak*, where all these drunken noblemen were shouting for all they're worth, "*Long live Sir Watkyn!*" What an Eisteddfod of Mockery.[72] What a Feast of Fools.

If Sir Watkyn should give all the money he spent on drink and carousing either to support the children of the poor in schools where they might learn a trade, or to reduce his rents, it would all be incomparably better. But instead, it's *raising* rents they're carrying on with! O! the compassion of it all!

June 1st: Here begins a new month, the sixth of the year.

May was remarkably pleasant and almost entirely warm. The only problem was that it was also cruelly dry. But at least there was favorable weather for carrying on with our work, such as hauling more than 20 barrels of lime over from Newtown. As a result, the field and the sheepwalk and the mountain pasture all appear quite fine.

June 3rd: We're sowing rutabegas and turnips.

I read at night – about the debate in the House of Commons concerning the sugar duty; the timber duty; and, especially, the corn duty. Inhabitants of the towns and the laborers are calling for the corn duty to be repealed, so that bread will be more affordable. I myself am waffling between two points of view,[73] and I ponder the matter this way:

1. Inexpensive bread is a great blessing, of course. But,

2. If bread is inexpensive, how can we farmers pay rent to our landlords…when they don't reduce their rents? Cheaper bread than our own will flood in from foreign countries, and there'll be no one left to want *our* bread. We'll be compelled to stop growing wheat. That's the only choice we'll have. More and more, in other words, we'll be putting tillage of the land aside. *A fatal stroke for agriculture.*

3. What about the farm workers? When we stop tilling, what work will be left for them? None at all. There'll be no great need for anyone to plough, to spread manure, to turn the soil and dig, to sow, to reap, to thresh. What benefits will cheap bread offer them when they won't have a penny to pay for it? Do we mean to sweep them out of the countryside and into the towns, into the factories…or off to 'Merica? These are bleak prospects, *at best*.

4. And what about all the rural trades? The smiths and the builders – both carpenters and masons – the millers, the weavers, the cobblers and the tailors? Who will give *them* work? And if they don't work, who will keep them alive? If agriculture dies, they too will die, as will all of their artisanship and all of their skills. It will be the *death of talent, the death of excellence, the death of every rural art*. The sweet sounds that fill even the smallest villages with harmony will fade away. Those noises and activities interwoven into the pattern of a Welshman's life – that actually collude in supporting and maintaining Welsh Society – all of them will be dead and gone.

Are the people who seek, so single-mindedly, to improve their lot taking everything into consideration? Are these people really so unconcerned with others' circumstances?

June 10th: It's the saddest news of all – John Elias…has…died! At eleven o'clock last Tuesday night, the 8th of the month, with his family at *y Bron*,[74] in Llangefni. The pious and gifted John Elias has left the stage.

I think about never again seeing his dignified head with its broad brow, his tall body and long arms – and especially, his eyes… the flames of his eyes! What will you be, Bala Assembly, without John Elias?

Never again will his thunder be heard upon your mountain! A man of God has departed. Just like *Elias*, the ancient prophet,[75] he has been exalted into heaven.

JUNE 21ST:[76] A letter – from a member of that troop that left here for 'Merica in April. It's interesting. He arrived there on the first of this month; and he had "a comfortable sea-journey," he says. "Not very bad weather at all, although an occasional wave did scatter over us and cast us one atop the other." There were 260 on the ship, "171 of us genuine Welshmen, from both the South and the North." He continues in a bit more detail:

"*The first afternoon, it was decided that we would hold religious services in this way: To worship every morning at 10, and in the afternoon at 7; and to hold some council meetings on such matters as Temperance, how to behave, how to speak, etc.… Also two sermons every Sunday for the Welsh, at 2 and 7; and one for the English at 11.*

"*Upon reaching the Banks of Newfoundland, 129 of the Welshmen pledged themselves to be Temperance-men in the new country. An Association of Purity was formed amongst the Youth, and 34 of their number pledged themselves. Also, a Society against Tobacco. We reached Newfoundland in 12 days, where we saw mountains of ice; and we've seen many wonders upon the great deep – whales, countless great fishes.*

"*On Monday the 31st, we rose very early expecting to see land. At about 7, land came into view. Even the feeblest amongst us took on a new sort of disposition, all at once. We couldn't even express our feelings; and if ever we were thankful to the Lord from the bottom of our hearts for His goodness to us, I'm sure we were at that time – and many of us were in tears.*

"*At about 12 the next day, we put our feet upon the soil of America, the 1st day of June, 1841: It's a day we'll remember for the rest of our lives.*"

How like the story of my uncle Edward who, along with Ezekiel Hughes, sailed to the same place in 1795! They, too, with their daily religious services. *One* daily service; and there wasn't any talk then about Temperance and Purity and Anti-Tobacco. *Wales in 1795: Wales in 1841!*

J<small>UNE</small> 22ND: I read the story of John Elias' funeral…and spend a lot of time mulling it over. I can see him as if I had been there myself.

The night before the funeral (the 15th of this month, one week ago), a sermon was delivered in Llangefni by the Rev. W. Roberts, of Amlwch. The congregation was huge; and they were so overcome by grief that they couldn't sing the Hymns that had been put out for the occasion. Roberts' topic was, "*Where is the Lord God of Elias* [i.e., Elijah]*?*" How very appropriate.

The next morning, at about 9 o'clock, the body was borne out of the house into the hearse, and the Rev. H. Griffiths of Llandrygarn addressed the multitude with a somber and interesting speech. John Elias had chosen to be buried in Llanfaes, and the funeral procession formed throughout the morning.

It was a long journey, about 15 miles; and all along the route, people showed the greatest signs of respect for the departed Saint. All work stopped everywhere the procession passed; every window was veiled; every man and woman was either in the funeral procession or looking out for it – hundreds of bystanders lined the entire route, at turn after turn of the road.

Between 12 and 1 o'clock, the great procession approached Menai Bridge, where even more troops stepped up, so that you would have marveled at the length, the number of the followers and the order that prevailed. At the front were the hosts that had joined in, one after another, from Llangefni to the Bridge – there were now thousands of men and women on foot, four-abreast; and behind them all were the four doctors who had attended to John Elias in his affliction. The hearse bearing the coffin and the members of the immediate family followed in four carriages. Then, 12 ministers on horseback, two-by-two; and 150 horsemen in twos as well – amongst them were virtually every preacher in Anglesey.

The procession wound its way forward in all its melancholy, through the village of Borth and up to a finger of the Menai River where the tide neither ebbed nor flowed. On the approach to Garth, numerous groups from Bangor filed in – groups that had carefully crossed over the Straits in ships with flags at half-mast as a sign of all Bangor's mourning. Even as they stretched out, the ranks of the mournful procession continued to fill, and they moved forward with heavy steps, somberly and slowly towards Beaumaris.

The leading group descended towards the cloister which stands between the sea and the old town, and there the Singers of Bangor had formed themselves into one great choir. They began singing Funeral Hymns as the myriad mourners filed past on the way towards town. Evidence of solemnity and sadness, mourning and respect was everywhere on display throughout Beaumaris. Every shop was closed; every window darkened; and every soul in town had gathered in the streets to watch and to marvel. The procession turned up towards the Church, where the Rev. Henry Griffith read the burial service, assisted by the Rev. H. Jones, curate of Llanfaes. Thousands of eyes watched them through streaming tears.

The host started off again, and the vanguard wound past the Castle, along the seashore and up through the verdure of field and foliage until reaching that place of peace, Llanfaes, where this beloved son of our nation was buried in full view of a multitude that continued to swell until the very end. A greater number was never seen, even at a Revival Meeting in Bala.

That incomparable procession was wonderful to behold, as it started out and its ranks swelled, thickened, twisted and straightened, ascended and descended throughout that long, long summer's day. Wonderful, too, was the way it later unmade itself, as ranks and troops peeled away at village after village, home after home. A host of people returned to Bangor after the burial, where a funeral sermon was delivered by the Rev. J. Foulkes, of Abergele, upon this passage from Hebrews 13:7[77] – *"Keep in mind your elders…"* The innumerable crowd seemed a flood of solemnity.

There you have it: another one of those days associated with John Elias! It almost makes me believe that John Elias' death stands out as the principal phenomenon of our time!

JUNE THE 25TH: One of the great *inventions* of our time is the train. The railroad has yet to reach Powys, but we hear a lot about it – and about how convenient it is for trade and travel. Hurry, let us praise every new contraption!

People predict that the train which runs through Taff Vale will transform Merthyr and Cardiff into a single great town! And today, I read about someone named Robert Davies in Merthyr getting his dinner from Cardiff – and it was, someone said, as warm as if it had just come out of the oven! The next thing you know they'll be making dinner on the train itself, likely enough.

JULY 1ST: June has departed once more, and the wheel keeps turning. June, with all its growth and charm, was particularly cheerful and warm this year. And May, beforehand, was almost equally pleasant.

It seems a sin to mention any fault concerning either month – namely, that they were much too dry. The crops will be scant and underweight this year, even if we do have a fairly good harvest.

"We can put all that hay, yonder, in my empty pocket," said Dafydd Dafis, *y Gytros*.[78] "Look at what a deuce of skimpiness it is!" He's always making mischief, that one.

July the 2nd: The *Temperance Festival of Llanidloes* took place yesterday and today. Since it's still a bit early for mowing hay, I decided to go – got there by nine in the morning, having set out on my pony at six. As I arrived, so did all the other Temperance-men of the surrounding districts. There were five speeches at the nine o'clock meeting.

At one o'clock, a procession formed out of the crowds just then exiting the chapels, and it joined ranks with the Rechabite Society[79] from Temperance House. There were about 2,000 people in all!

We marched through all the streets of the town, and headed for the Speaker's Platform. There were three good speeches and more of the same at 6 o'clock.

Without a doubt, one of the best Festivals we've had since the Society was founded. Everyone was very satisfied!

July the 3rd: The weather has finally broken. It's wet and cold. Farther down the shire, a lot of hay is on the ground. We, however, haven't yet started to mow in order to give it a chance to grow a little while longer. And the entire countryside is a-boil over the election. What a jumble of confounded opinions. O! the Chartists are likely to give their vote to the Tories!

July the 10th: Today the judge arrives at Newtown for the Court of Assizes – and tomorrow old Gwallter Mechain will preach there, as the High Sheriff's chaplain.

JULY THE 14TH: It's still cold, and on some days it's wet all day long. The scythes and the sledges and the great wagons and everything else are all ready for haying – everything, that is, except the weather! A good season for ducks, though…and for an Election!

JULY THE 15TH: Mid-month, and the weather's so unstable.

I read a bit in *The Treasury* – full of good pieces, both light-hearted and serious. There's a letter by the Rev. D. Morgan, of Welshpool, decrying the "great battle" between Lewis Edwards and Sam Roberts. He wants them *"to put the debate to one side, henceforth; and to stop writing on these dry and inflammatory subjects; they should use their excellent talents to write about more appealing and important topics than the Nature of the Church, etc., etc."*

I agree with him; and I have said as much to Sam Roberts on more than one occasion.

But what's with this Morgan fellow and his decision to conclude his letter in French – "in a language," even he admits, "that not everyone will recognize"? As far as that goes, wouldn't he achieve the same effect with English? Even amongst readers of *The Treasury*, scarcely one in ten can understand an English passage. Well, anyway… here's what he says:

"*Je suis très faché* [sic], *mes chers freres* [sic], *de tout l'embarras que vous vous êtes donnés…Abandonnez, je vous prie, ces sujets désagréables qui ne tiennent à rien de bon…Il ya* [sic] *des sujets de plus grande importance que le contrat constitutionnel des Methodistes* [sic], *et la nature du gouvernement de l'église…*

"*C'est pourquoi, Je vous conjure d'employer vos talents, vos affections, vos mains, de quelque chose plus profitable…*

"*J'ai l'honneur d'etre* [sic] *votre très humble et très obéissant Serviteur, et votre très sincere ami.*

"*Dans l'union de l'Evangile. – D. Morgan*"

["I am quite annoyed, my dear brothers, with all the embarrassment you have caused…Abandon, I pray you, these disagreeable subjects which pertain to nothing good…There are subjects of far greater importance than the constitutional charter of the Methodists and the nature of church governance…

"That's why I beg you to devote your talents, your interests, your hands to something more profitable…

"I have the honor of being your very humble and very obedient Servant, and your very true friend.

"Together in Evangelism. – D. Morgan."]

JULY 17: I see a story about the Court of Assizes in Newtown. There wasn't a single prisoner in the dock; nothing but petty cases. Let's waste no more time – we must proclaim for all to hear: See what progress the world has made!

And here's a short but quite interesting letter from a daughter of Gwallter Mechain to her Mother, in which she describes circumstances in town and at court. It's shame it's in English[80]…but still worth reading:

"*Newtown, 12th July 1841:*

"*Dear Mamma. On Saturday set off in a chariot and four from Crosswood about 10 o'clock to New Town; went through Pool* [Welshpool] *sheep and pig fair: at Newtown by 12. Mr. Davies of Vronvelen called, and Mr. and Mrs. Buckley Williams and Miss Williams. The Church yesterday crowded; they were standing in crowds outside the doors and windows, and all the aisles filled. Papa got through the sermon very well – looks well, and hopes that you are well, and then all will be well. The Sheriff and his Chaplain dined yesterday at 6 o'clock at Newtown Hall, to meet the Judge; – the Bar did not arrive in time to go there. Lord Abinger, the Judge, they say is a very agreeable personage. My father dines with him at his lodgings at 7 this evening; Mr. Vaughan presides at the Grand Jury dinner today. Lord Powis sent on Saturday half a buck, a present to the Sheriff, – but a haunch of venison will be sent to the Grand Jury dinner; the other half of the buck was sent for the Judge. Mrs. Vaughan and I sat yesterday at Church in the Newtown Hall pew, and the Judge and the Sheriff sat in one close by…We did not know where to go, when the verger met us and took us to that seat…*

"We are quite safe, the 2ⁿᵈ Battalion of the Rifle Brigade are stationed here;(!) there is not one prisoner for trial – but some causes…only 40 spectators to be admitted. We have had our ticket to go from the Under Sheriff." [81]

Fearing for her life, the little minx…in Newtown! Is that the explanation for those soldiers?

JULY 18ᵀᴴ: Sunday. We head out for Chapel, everybody save one; and the day is quite fair – in the midst of this cold, wet spell. I run into Dafydd Dafis, *y Gytros,* on my way to chapel.

"It's a fine morning, Dafydd Davis."

"'Tis, 'tis. 'Tis Sunday, is it not? I'll warrant He takes the trouble to make *His* day a good 'un!"

That's Dafydd for you – downright pagan even on Sundays and feast days.

JULY 19ᵀᴴ: We tackle the hay-mowing. Five scythes go at it, all day long. Mowing in five directions. The hay's pretty scanty.

JULY 24: The end of a serious week of haying. The weather is very unpleasant. We get several loads in, though, almost as if on the sly.

JULY 31: Another week, and it's cold and showery. It's wearing out the hay and leaving it in fairly poor condition. There won't be any smell or sap or flavor to it. It's looking like a bland, tasteless winter for the animals.

AUGUST THE 2ND: Too wet for haying. Disappointing weather. I send the boys to Waun Goch, near Bugeilyn, to fetch some loads of peat – there's as much need for a warm fire just now as in the dead of winter. It's a difficult journey, climbing those mountains. It's more difficult yet bringing full loads over steep slopes without toppling the trolleys on the way down. A single trip takes an entire day!

AUGUST THE 3RD: There's one of our Occasional Assembly Meetings in Machynlleth. It started yesterday, but I go down today since this is no weather for haying. I'll make it in time for the Deacons' Meeting, anyway. I get there, and town's full of outsiders.[82]

To the meeting, where we deal with these matters:

- Paying off the debt for the Houses of Worship – our accounts are fairly encouraging.
- Sunday School. Attendance is increasing, but too slowly. It's noted that many inhabitants of the countryside aren't members. In this shire alone, more than 30,000 have never been to Sunday School. Who would have thought? Worse yet: many people, especially the poorest, don't know how to read the first word in a book. Nation of the Gospel, indeed!
- It's also noted that some of the people attending Sunday School, at certain locations, are very rude, like mindless beasts. We agree that there's a need for the Pulpit to pay more attention to Sunday School – by emphasizing its value to religion, to good manners and to culture. We need to raise its profile throughout the countryside.

- *The Day of Sabbath*. We acknowledge that it's being defiled ever more frequently in some districts – sometimes by inappropriate conversation; sometimes by spending too much attention on meals; sometimes by excessive preoccupation with one's personal appearance; or sometimes by reading unprofitable books and monthly publications, which should be set aside for another day.

We conclude that the Sabbath is a very valuable day, a day to be spent entirely in God's cause – but we also acknowledge that one can't be blamed for wearing better clothes or having a somewhat nicer meal, because the activities of this Day should be, by all rights, of better quality than those of any other day.

August 4th: Perverse weather, and many hayfields are battered down – in several places they're rotting. We smuggle an occasional load into the loft, even so. We're not working; we're getting worked over.

August the 10th:[83] The hay harvest is still both troublesome and exhausting – what's more, the days are getting shorter.[84]

I run an errand over in Darowen village. The parson lets me borrow an issue of *The Sun*, and he tells me there's a story about the death of John Elias in it, along with praise for his life's work. I place it under my armpit and take it home. What does it have to say about John Elias? Was John Elias always favorably disposed to the [Anglican] church? Did he feel something like dear kinship with it?

I open to the story. Here we are:

"One of the most wonderful men whose name has ever been associated with the religious history of the Principality…He served the Methodist Body for 27 years, and he descended into the grave still dignified by his striking white head of hair."

Let's hear it for *The Sun*!

August the 13th: Cold and fierce, and the wind moans through the ears of grain in the fields, and through gaps in the stone walls. Field after field of hay blown down and scattered about. It's heartbreaking!

But things are hardly better at the Factory Works, it's said. There's been a 10-percent reduction in wages for the laborers at Dowlais and thereabouts; bread and food are expensive. "We're emigrating," say the laborers. "We're emigrating," say the farmers. Everyone wants to emigrate! *One* thing's increasing in Dowlais – the number of pubs! Fifteen years ago, there wasn't but one pub. Today, 200 of them!

August 17th: The weather's improving, and signs are that it will continue to do so. What an abrupt change since yesterday and the day before. O, Providence! I hope it stays pleasant for several days – for weeks even. That's our only chance to finish some sort of hay harvest before everything rots where it stands. The grain is already knocking at the door. So is the peat. We could do with a month of dryness. Then, the whole harvest can be brought in yet again – and we can bury all that nonsense about emigrating.

August 25th: I wished that it would come, and it has – good weather! Excellent conditions for a whole week. Every load of hay put away snug. Bless the Heavens. The scythes at work again, and some sickles too.[85] The grain is calling; we're ready. Let's get to it!

August 28th: We're reaping throughout the day, 20 of us. A dumpling for dinner; flummery and milk for supper.

Then, I read a letter from my cousin in 'Merica. It's Wm. Bebb himself, son of my uncle Edward who emigrated in 1795.[86] William is 39 years old now, and he's a successful attorney in Hamilton, Ohio. For 20 years, he's been writing occasionally to my brother and me – in

English, although he can understand and speak Welsh as well as I can. Shame on him!

This letter was written on the 6th of August. He spent a long time, he says, traveling widely throughout parts of the United States "looking for land for my sister's children, and investing the money that was sent to me from Wales." In Long Prairie, he ran across our other cousin, E.B. Jones, of Cwmpenllydan, along with his family – everyone's healthy and prosperous. Jones had eight men digging a two-mile-long canal through his property.

There's a full account of his journey – four pages long – in black ink and then, later, in blue ink. That's American frugality for you!

He provides a lot of information about different parts of the country, as well as observations and advice:

> *Indiana* and *Illinois* – good lands, but the two states are in debt.
> *Iowa* – Very good, but the "squatters" are seizing land there by violence.
> *Missouri* – lots of good land…*"but slavery has thrown her withering curse over that state and you would not go there of course."*
> *Wisconsin* – too far north, and the winters are long and cold.
> *Ohio* – better than the others, and he's quite partial to it.

He complains that money has been scarce in this latter place for two years, but things are improving. He concludes this way:

"I lately received a letter from cousin Samuel Roberts,[87] *and I will write to him soon…I perceive by the papers that the Tories have defeated the Whigs of Great Britain in the elections; and what surprises me, that the Chartists voted with the Tories. I understand perhaps as little of the state of your parties there as you do*

of the difficulties attending the ABOLITION OF SLAVERY *in the United States"…*
–Wm. Bebb

SEPTEMBER THE 1ST: There's been a debate in Parliament over the Queen's Speech, and the Whigs have been forced to resign from office. The Tories will govern next; and more than likely, Robert Peel[88] will lead. Birds of a feather are they all.

SEPTEMBER THE 8TH: Yesterday, today, tomorrow – the Association Meeting at Bangor. The keynote event will be the funeral sermon for John Elias by the preacher Henry Rees of Liverpool.

It's futile for me to think about going, what with the weather being this fine and the grain only half-reaped. The harvesting is so easy, and we're at it day and night. Thanks to the sun and the frost, the grain has finished ripening; and the warmth dries it as it stands in sheafs!

The fields are full of reapers, both men and women; and the house is seething with the preparation of food at all hours of day. The jolly, cheerful dance of harvest-tide.

SEPTEMBER THE 18TH: Almost finished with the grain.

Machynlleth Fair is held today. It's a major sheep fair. When I arrive, thousands of sheep are already here; and the town is flooded with their bleating, the barking of dogs and the hollering of shepherds. The streets of Maengwyn, Penyrallt and Pentre-rhedyn are boiling furiously with commotion, which spills down into the Garrison, over to the Tollhouse and out towards Graigfach and Maesglas.

There's more fuming than bartering taking place. Sales are slow, and prices are low. Just past noon, the shepherds drive their sheep home again, and all the commotion and jostling vanish completely. The farmers, though, loiter about, gathering at the Hall to catch up with one another – to talk about the good weather we've been having for a month now, about the scarcity of hay and grain, about pangs and distresses of every sort…and about letters from *'Merica*.

The old town is suddenly as quiet as usual; and the cooks and maids are fetching water from the spring at Pistyll Gwyn, whereas the children of the Garrison use the Garrison's own spring instead. And behold, there's Sir John Edwards of Plas Machynlleth. That congenial old bird is spreading his wings about the town with his loyal retainer Edward Llywelyn at his side, as usual. The two are the same age, I think. But Sir John's mane isn't as red as it once was. They turned him out at the recent Election after roughing him up a bit!

I run an errand or two in Tomas the Pharmacist's shop, then mount the pony and head for home. A very clever man is Tomas.

SEPTEMBER 24TH: The majority of the grain is safely gathered in. We're gleaning the stubble. We bring home more peat, not from Waun Goch this time – thank goodness! – but from the nearby moor!

It's Friday night – Fellowship Meeting. I make my way there on the double. Two of the village tailors went out gathering nuts last Sunday instead of attending Sunday School. The ministers amongst the membership want to be easy on them:

"That's the first time they've transgressed…," they say.

"One time too many," I reply. "It's necessary to confront sin in earnest, so as not to sanction offence."

In the end, we all agree…to conclude the meeting. And to think we're worried about discipline!

SEPTEMBER 25TH: I set the boys to finish gleaning the grain fields and stacking the peat.

Another sheep fair in Machynlleth. I go look it over. A lot less crowded than the previous one. People know how futile it is to drive sheep over a long distance and then have to herd them back afterwards. Just plain disheartening is what it is.

I call in at Ffowc Ifans' shop – he's a much better shopkeeper than a preacher, that's for sure! I catch a glimpse of the cunning Tomas Huws. There's something like a guilty look about him, on account of talk he's been expelled from the Monthly Meetings – for his stern opposition to hard drink, as he'd have you believe. A chick for his Sunday dinner and a drop of small beer – that's Tomas Huws' ideal. And a bowlful of posset[89] when there's nothing better to hand! "Tomas Huws of Machynlleth…has been cut off from Session Meetings! Yes, he's been cut off from Monthly Meetings…and from the fellowship of the Church of the Methodists!" That's how he portrays it, anyway. And then he adds: "Tomas Huws of Machynlleth…has been cut off from the Book of the Lamb![90]…But, no…they can't do that, can they! Dare they?" And everyone will weep, and Tomas Huws will get his second chance!

SEPTEMBER 26TH: Sunday – and the weather has broken. There'll be rain now.

To Chapel. Dafydd Davies of Cywarch is preaching. Reproachful, and very radical. A Temperance Sermon, as usual.

Back home for dinner. Then to Llan Darowen in the afternoon and home again for a supper of flummery. It's too late to be setting out for evening meeting afterwards, but I do anyway. The small chapel is full, and every seat on the benches is taken. The singing is remarkably good.

Back to the house, after walking about 12 miles – the same thing every Sunday. For me, this is the hardest day of all!

SEPTEMBER 28TH: Wet and harsh. I write a letter to my cousin in *'Merica*. I want a lot more explanation about the states over there, the produce of the land, etc. Two thoughts keep nagging me when I contemplate the idea of emigrating. Is it a rational thing to do? More importantly, is it a Scriptural thing to do?

October the 15th: The weather is cursed. There's a layer of snow all over the landscape, and it lies thick upon the summits of Cader Idris and Aran Mawddwy. A white world, already. Cold enough for snow at harvest season! And we haven't even gotten the bracken in yet!

Here we are, facing months of hard times. Scarcity and high prices and poverty throughout the countryside. I read about two poor women fined half a crown for gleaning in the field of some fellow, Owen Roberts of Bwlan. Isn't gleaning one of the traditions of the Welsh countryside? And isn't Scripture emphatic about leaving the gleaning for the poor – *"leaveth them for the poor,"* says Leviticus xxiii:22.

October 21: Machynlleth Sheep Fair today – and a "new" fair at Dinas Mawddwy tomorrow. I can hardly afford to go to both of them this year. Since I have other errands to do there, I ride to Machynlleth. For the most part, the snow is gone; but the breezes are stinging, and the streams and rivers more than fill their beds. The entire countryside looks sad and miserable.

Maengwyn Street is hardly busier than on a typical day. There are a few more souls around Town Hall, and more yet to the right and the left towards Penyrallt and Pentre-rhedyn. There's an occasional ungainly flock grazing alone on the commons of the Park. There's no enthusiasm at all in evidence amongst either sheep or dogs or shepherds. Dafydd Dafis, *y Gytros*, is lamenting to no one in particular:

"A month ago, you could've trampled that moor yonder into hard earth, so parched and bare it was ... Today, it'd be dangerous for a man to wander out into it for fear of drowning hisself."

Glimpses of Life in Wales

· · · · ·

On the way home, I remember that today is my birthday. I'm 54 years old. Whom do I believe in? What do I work for? A deacon for 30 years, walking to Chapel thrice each Sunday, Prayer Meetings on Tuesday nights, Assembly Meetings on Friday nights. I discipline myself severely day in, day out. I discipline everyone around me – the wife, the children, the farm hands and maids, church members, smokers and drinkers, naughty children and people who haven't come to religion. I'm an overseer of "rules" and laws.

Everyone respects me – out of fear. Who loves me? To what purpose have I harassed everyone…have I harassed myself?

OCTOBER THE 28TH: The shepherd has just brought over a load of rushes for making candles. It's a bit of work for the girls to peel them carefully, so that they leave one strip in place that keeps the middle – or the heart – from breaking. After they're peeled, they go into a long pan full of tallow. And then the rushes are transformed into candles! We keep them all together in a special small dispenser[91] under the mantle, and we use them one-by-one, night after night, all winter long. A peat fire below, the light of rush candles in the kitchen – now those are the makings of a comfortable hearthside.

OCTOBER 30TH: The boys are moving a crate-full of oats from the grain rick to the barn, and they start to thresh it. The cattle will soon be inside for the winter, and the custom is to thresh a goodly portion of the oats *before* bringing them in. That's what will preoccupy the lads for the next week. Then, we'll take it in saddle bags to the mill for grinding. Milling day is a pretty important occasion for us.

NOVEMBER 3RD: We're floundering about trying to cut and gather bracken…for weeks now. We're wet right through to the skin;

and it's ruining the horses, all that dragging of sledges through wet moorland day after day. In the end, we manage to haul a fair number of loads back to the corn rick. Hardly enough by a long shot, of course; but it's good to have what we've got. Having a dry bed of ferns under them will be of considerable help to the animals throughout the winter.

NOVEMBER THE 8TH: Daylight shortens with each passing day, and the weather continues to get colder. Shelter and warmth are the first requirements for both man and beast – we're either in the stable, the cowshed, the granary or the "timber house" doing chores all day long. Then, at nightfall, I block out the wind and the rain and the snow all round us, and we huddle by the peat fire – my mother in the armchair; myself and one or two of the children in the corner; one or two of the maids on the "*setl*" [settle]. There are three-legged stools for everyone else. Everyone has their tasks – the girls at the large spinning wheel [for wool] and the small one [for flax], or knitting stockings; the boys carving, making ropes, wooden spoons and handles for the spades and pitchforks. Mother knits yarn with her hands, stories with her tongue – stories about old Wales in days long gone; about the Vigils and Funeral Services at ancient burials; about the *Tylwyth Teg* [Fairy Family] that inhabited the slopes of Newydd Fynyddog [near Dolfach and Llanidloes]; about the old games played when she was a lass; and about the famous cock-fight in Llanbrynmair in 1795, when the cockerel of Siôn the Goldsmith, from Aberhosan, defeated rival cockerels from all over the district. The stories follow one after another; and as she finishes each yarn, the children call out, "Come again, Nain [Grandmother]!" They positively rejoice to hear the old tales and all those fantastical exploits.

NOVEMBER THE 13TH: Old *Calan Gaeaf,* [92] and Mother's in the mood to tell stories about the spirit world – even though she doesn't believe a single word of them. I myself am trying to read – at the moment, a very impressive article on "The U*n*patriotism of the Welsh." The author is urging the use of Welsh names for children, and Welsh words on signs for inns and shops, and on gravestones. And for Pubs and Taverns! It would be better if these latter had neither signs *nor* locations. And who's the author? "A Prosperous Welshman," he says, "who wears his own wool and brews his own beer, whose kitchen serves Welsh mutton and whose wife and daughters wear Welsh clothes that they make for themselves…." I sympathize with every word…except for the brewing. At its best, a farm is a small, fully-matured kingdom – an extended family living within its own productive, peaceful realm. It's heaven on earth – so long as justice prevails!

NOVEMBER 16TH: One week ago, a son was born to the queen. There's been meaningless rejoicing ever since. Thousands of our fellow-countrymen in Wales are half-starving; and their cold lamentations, of course, are hardly able to drown out such declarations of joy over the birth of a prince!

He will be a Prince of Wales, I warrant; and there's much debate about giving him a Welsh name, like Cadwaladr or Llywelyn. A right good thing…I suppose; although a name won't change his spots.

Others are debating the establishment of two Chairs of Welsh[93] – now there's an idea! Others yet are arguing about the role the Welsh flag should play at important occasions. Very noble sentiments, but they're still just crumbs.

December 7: More talk about dire circumstances throughout the countryside. There's scarcity of money, a slump in commerce and trade... and, yes, hunger and nakedness too.

Many keep carrying on about the Corn Laws being the principal cause of all our distress. The "League for the Abolition of the Corn Laws" holds meeting after meeting "to enlighten the common folk," as they like to say. They plead their case and arouse the countryside. They cry out for petitions to be drafted and signed – in every shire, city, town, village, neighborhood and district.

They recently held one of their large meetings at Caernarfon. Hundreds and hundreds of people attended, it's said; and the meeting went on for three or four days – it may not be over yet, in fact.

Many Ministers of the Gospel – especially amongst the Independents and the Baptists – have spoken and preached there. They scream, "Rise up! Rise up! Rise up!" until they witness the fruits of their exhortations. Then they're the first to disavow the uprisings! Someone ought to knot one or two of their tongues.

December 9th: Another long letter from my cousin – in two colors of ink, one over the other, as usual. Such a fine web to behold; such a genuine challenge to read.

He's answering the letter I wrote on the 28th of September. Once again, he took a long sweep through the country, looking for land "suitable for my sister and our friends in Wales." He's also looking for land to invest in with the money he's received from Wales, because paper money in *'Merica* is suffering devaluation.

He set out on horseback the 27th of October, sometimes riding as far as 38 miles a day. He came upon the farm of "our friend from Wales, Griffith Breeze, to the south of Lima [Ohio]. Then to the Welsh settlement at Ottawa (*"on Hog Creek"*), and to Vanwert. Onward to "*E.B. Jones' Praire.*" "Everyone there is well and prospering. By now, there are 35 families in the settlement, and roads cross it from every direction. A tempest of wind and rain blew up, and trees fell about our heads everywhere. A narrow escape. I stayed in a cabin and had a supper of *'mush and milk.'"* He didn't care for the land around there. Farther on, the land was level and rich, but there was no spring or brook or stream. He reached a cabin belonging to Indians; it was open on every side but one and had a roof of bark. He encamped there one night and saw lots of deer, but failed to get near enough to shoot one.

He gathered a bed of leaves from the nearby woods and slept fairly well. He headed out towards Indiana the following day and spent the night with a *"raw Yankee family"*...whose children were *"showing all the simplicity and curiosity of untutored youth."* He was one of 14 who slept in the wooden cabin, next to a great fire. The next day, there came a great snow; and it was cold. Then he headed back to the county seat of Vanwert, after making sure there was no land thereabouts "suitable for my sister or for you." Back at E.B. Jones' place, he bought some of that land for Ann and Jane Jones, *"giving them the preference as they are ladies."* He decided not to buy any more until next summer. Meantime, he was saving money, without loaning any of it out to other buyers. He was afraid we wouldn't get our money back when it came time for the other buyers to sell.

He turned for home and called in on Griffith Breeze again. When he reached Lima and Harding, he was feeling rather poorly. Fainting spells – due to an excess of fatigue and hunger, wet feet and sleeping out in the open. At chapel on Sunday, he heard Mr. Hale preaching: "Death is physical as far as the mind is concerned; life and peace are spiritual."

Across: [94] an explanation of the monetary devaluation in the United States since 1836, with lots of blame for General Andrew

Jackson's decision to flood the country with local banks, etc. But now, having passed through much distress, the country is making steps towards prosperity.

"We have the best land on earth and an incomparable people for performing thrifty toil. Therefore, this country, by the grace of God, simply must succeed.

"A word in reply to your questions: If you decide to come to 'Merica, it would be better for you to wait three or four years until more land is opened up and cleared. You're not well suited for Woodlands, and you wouldn't find yourself comfortable there for many years. I well know what sort of land you want, though it's a lot easier to describe it than to acquire it at present…

"As concerns the complaints of those who have left here to return to Wales, I suppose there might be some justification for their decision. I believe the verdure[95] *– the green grass of England and Wales is greener than that of America – Your damp climate, your cloudy weather, your constant rains, promote the freshness of your meadows – while our brilliant skies and bright sunshine and frequent droughts…burn up our grass. Yet our Timothy grass meadows are not excelled by any…*

"There is no OATMEAL *in the U. States – and that is because wheat flour is better and cheaper. Besides, if you must have coarse meal, Indian corn is…a* CHEAPER *and better article(!!)"* And so forth, etc.

He concludes with some family news – his mother is alive and well (the sister of John Roberts of Llanbrynmair, that is). His brother is still in New York. His sister is having trouble with her eyes. He himself has four children, *"all promising and good children."* His work is prospering splendidly – he'll take in 3,000 dollars this year!

"When I write so long a letter as this, I intend it, of course, for you – for all who sent me money. I have not time to write to all such long letters. – Show

it also to Cousin Samuel [96]. – Tell him I recd his kind letter, and present to all relatives…my kindest love.

"*I remain, dear cousins, yours ever,* – WM. BEBB"

Despite his length, he doesn't address all that I want to know. Also, there's too much praise for *'Merica*. The land that's been opened up is very expensive, and the rest requires quite an arm for cutting and clearing trees. Here I am over 50 years old. Could I possibly start over and face such punishing labor? I have children, it's true; but only two are boys.

My mind is thoroughly bewildered and perplexed. I've felt the same way for years and years. Is it legitimate to do such a thing? Is it scriptural? Heavenly Father, it is You who provide me with certainty about every other thing. But not about this. "Cut away the doubt that so discomfits…"

DECEMBER 14TH: I read in the paper that the Pope has become a Temperance-man. How virtuous indeed is this Pope! And let no Protestant think the worse of Temperance for the Pope's having embraced it.

DECEMBER THE 17TH: A great storm, with lightning and thunder and giant, prodigious hailstones – about three inches around. I watch the lightning flash for what seems like ages. It's a wonderful yet dreadful display. And the noise is horrendous. The lightning stabs; the thunder peals. Tongues of fire; torrents of cloudburst – the wonderful splendor of the heavens "declaring the glory of God…" Upon these hills, we are like watchmen looking down upon the tempest in the valleys and the gorges, in the vales, over the precipices. What sort of damage is being done there, in town and village, house and cowshed? I head home to comfort the children.

December the 20th: My fears have come to pass. Word is that lightning has struck many cowsheds here and there and killed a lot of cattle. In several places, houses have been completely demolished.

What's more, accounts of misery and penury abound; the salary of many a worker in Wales is but sixpence a day – sixpence, and perhaps a meal. And from that sixpence, he's supposed to pay rent and buy food and clothes for the wife and five or more of his children.

The coal works in Glamorgan and Monmouth are remarkably lifeless, and the inhabitants of these districts are plainly morose over their prospects as they face a winter now reaching full strength. The Chartists continue to hold the occasional meeting in the vicinity of Pont-y-pŵl, despite all the surveillance of their activities. Is it any wonder though, now that wages have been reduced by a shilling or more per pound of coal? It's being rumored that the laborers in Rhymney have refused to work and that they're pressing others nearby in Merthyr, Tredegar and Nant-y-glo to do the same. It's feared there'll be lots of rioting…again. And there's talk about sending in soldiers.

Things are similar in the North – never, I maintain, has work in the slate quarries been so dismal. I hear that the wharf at Bangor is piled high with stone, and there's no demand for it. Hordes of workers have already been turned out of their jobs. It's the onset of a calamity – in a region that's usually the most vibrant in all North Wales. At the onset of winter, no less.

December 24th: The night before Christmas. A night of vigil. Immediately after the milking, the girls get ready to make toffees. Suppertime is boisterous. And then, after taking a turn outdoors to look after the horses and cattle, the boys hurry back into the house – to give the girls a helping hand. The children are delighted, and the whole house is up on its feet to welcome the toffees.

December 31st: I begin the day with family chores and end it the same way. It's the best way to bid farewell to the old year – the only way, really.

And so: You've reached your end. I saw your worst more often than your best, your scowl more often than your smile. But I managed to live to see you buried, month by month, day by day, hour by hour. And I don't much long after you. Scarce was your abundance, abundant your scarcity.[97]

But I won't complain. I saw your better side now and then; I saw your worse side too, sometimes. And yet you allowed me to live through it all, and my family with me. I had some losses – with the sheep and the lambs, the hay and the grain. But the cowshed and the stable are mostly full; and the granary and the hayloft aren't as empty as I'd feared. Flitches of ham are hanging from the ridgepole, and there's no great lack of oat flour or cheese or butter. Why should I complain?

You fought hard against me. I fought back – just as hard. You reduced me to faint-heartedness at times; and you drove me, like a lot of my fellow Welshmen, to look for greener grass far to the other side of these dear, old hills. You didn't completely succeed; nor did you completely fail…more's the pity!

For 20 years now, my cousin has tried his level best to attract me to 'Merica. But bad years like you have been much better persuaders than he has ever been. You are all great tempters. You are the serpents in the garden. It's you who throttle and bruise the mind.

You are the persecutors, who want to chase us out of the land of our fathers. You – and the *landlords*. You and the landlords – and the *Church Tax*. You and the landlords and the Church Tax – and the

Tithe. You and the landlords and the Church Tax and the Tithe – and the *New Poor Law*. All of you and all of your kind: A curse on each and every one of you!

If I continue to vacillate, it's no thanks to you. It's thanks to your enemies – to my uncertainty concerning the will of God; to my unreadiness to pull up my roots from the soil where they've penetrated so deep; to my reluctance to cross the sea with some of the most uncivilized and ill-mannered Englishmen imaginable; to my doubts concerning prospects of leading a religious life over there; and, as much as anything else, to my affection for Wales, her language, her faith, her life. I dread to think of my family losing track of itself, like thousands upon thousands of other Welsh, dispersed throughout a sea of humanity of every nature and description such as exists over there.

I keep wavering – I've just read a letter intended for "the Welsh emigrants to America" by Hugh Evans of Talybont, near Abermaw. This is his message: "Now, my dear brothers, if you're unwilling to commingle with people of every tribe, language, nation and religion under heaven; if the nation of Wales is dear to you; *and if you are all for doing what you can to preserve the language that was entrusted by God to us as a nation* – you must unite to establish a Welsh Colony."

I'm wavering…under the spell of those concluding words: "the language that was entrusted by God to us as a nation." What would a Faraway Paradise be without her, without our blessed Welsh tongue?

• • • • •

William Bebb continued to waver until 1847, when he sailed with his wife and children, together with some other families from the same district, to Vanwert; and a son of his brother Edward, namely another William Bebb – my grandfather – escorted them in a wagon as far as Ruabon [below Wrexham, on their way, presumably, to their port of departure at Liverpool]. –*W.A. Bebb*

Notes to The Faraway Paradise

[1] Walter Davies (1761-1849); a poet of Llanfechain, Montgomeryshire. (See note 44 below.)

[2] Tomas Price (1787-1848); an antiquary based in Breconshire. (See note 44 below.)

[3] John Elias (1774-1841); Calvinistic Methodist minister, often referred to as "The Methodist Pope."

[4] John Jones (1796-1857); Calvinistic Methodist minister from Talysarn.

[5] William Rees (1802-1883); Denbighshire writer and editor.

[6] Samuel Roberts (1800-1885); Montgomeryshire minister, writer and Radical. From 1857-1867, S.R. settled in the Cumberland Plateau region of East Tennessee in the United States as a member of the ultimately unsuccessful Welsh colonizing settlement of *Brynyffynon*. (See note 87 below.)

[7] Meaning, "slope of rowan (or mountain ash) trees."

[8] Rev. Evan Jones was raised in the same district as Wm. Bebb; and an uncle of his, Ifan Jones of Maesteran, was a fellow deacon with Bebb from about 1815 to 1835. –*W.A. Bebb*

[9] Cf. Matthew 25:16 – "Then he that had received the five talents went and traded with the same, and made them other five talents."

[10] The Reform Bill of 1832, intended to allocate Members of Parliament more equitably and to broaden the electoral franchise among the Welsh.

[11] Emigrants from Wales established this town at the end of 1796, under the leadership of Rev. Rees Lloyd and George Roberts (brother of John Roberts, Llanbrynmair). At about the same time, the renowned Morgan John Rhys settled some three miles from there. –*W.A. Bebb*

[12] Letter is written in Welsh.

[13] The six parishes are Machynlleth, Cemaes, Llanwrin, Penegoes, Darowen and Llanbrynmair. –*W.A. Bebb*

[14] The followers of Alexander Campbell of Virginia.

[15] Roman Catholics.

[16] Also known as Presbyterians.

[17] *Gwynfyd fan draw*; literally, "Blessedness is over yonder."

[18] Chartism sought social and political reform throughout Great Britain in reaction to general economic depression; the ineffectiveness of the Reform Act of 1832; and revulsion against the New Poor Laws of 1834. Chartist agitation persevered from 1837 to 1844.

[19] John Frost (1784-1877), William Jones (1809-1873) and Zephaniah Williams (1795-1874). For their involvement in a violent skirmish in Newport (Gwent) on 4 November 1839, in which 22 were killed and some 50 wounded, this trio was sentenced to death. The sentence was later commuted to a life of exile in Van Dieman's Land (i.e., Tasmania). The sentence of banishment or "transportation" was also known as the Royal Mercy.

[20] John Elias (1774-1841), "the Methodist Pope." The Chartist movement at this time was divided amongst the "Moral Force" Chartists and the "Physical Force" Chartists.

[21] "Once the ox is killed, who will draw the plow?" In other words, killing the ox to eat now means foregoing one's opportunity to till the soil for future gain.

[22] One guinea equals 21 shillings, or £1 plus 1 shilling. A single Pound Sterling in 1841 would equate roughly to £70 ($110) today; and at 20 shillings to the pound, 1 shilling then would be the equivalent of about £3.50 ($5.60) now. A two-guinea prize, in other words, would be worth about £147 ($235).

²³ Rent of £80 represents about £5,600 ($8,960) of today's purchasing power.

²⁴ David Owen (1784-1841). (See note 41 below.)

²⁵ A prominent inn and public house in Machynlleth.

²⁶ Two guineas, yet again – or £147 ($235) today.

²⁷ Before marrying Wm. Bebb, she was Miss Margaret Owen, daughter of Dafydd and Lowri Owen of Y Faner, near Dolgellau. –*W.A. Bebb*

²⁸ "Bundling," or courting on a bed. (See note 66 below.)

²⁹ "'The Workhouse' – always a word of shame, grey shadow falling on the close of life, most feared by the old (even when called The Infirmary); abhorred more than debt, or prison, or beggary, or even the stain of madness." [from *Cider with Rosie*, Laurie Lee (Crown Publishers, 1984/1959), p. 102].

³⁰ Queen Victoria (1819-1901) was but 22 years old in 1841.

³¹ A Welshman.

³² Perhaps a sly pun is at work here: The translator has elected to render the obscure word *clydigaeth* (deriving from *clydo*, "to make comfortable") as "bearable". The similar sounding *cludo* means "to bear" or "to carry." How bearable was the bearing is left for the reader to decide.

³³ *Nos i nos a ddengys wybodaeth*. Note, as well, that this day represents the Celtic festival of Imbolc, a calendrical "cross-quarter" day denoting the ancient first day of Spring.

³⁴ A common word in this part of Montgomery for a narrow road or lane. –*W.A. Bebb* [Compare, also, the English word "outrake," which according to the *Oxford English Dictionary*, means "a free passage for sheep from inclosed (*sic*) pastures into open grounds, or common lands."] (See note 83, p. 175.)

³⁵ Soured oatmeal custard.

³⁶ "*Gwyn eu byd y tlodion*." A reference to "The Beatitudes" that begin with Matthew 5:3 – "Blessed are the poor in spirit…" (In Welsh, "*Gwyn eu byd y rhai s'yn dlodion yn yr ysbryd…*")

³⁷ The home of the Roberts family, in Dôl-fach. "Old" John Roberts was father to Samuel and "young" John, or J.R. (1804-1884). (See note 6 above.)

³⁸ Both of these Societies were in existence as early as 1838, because among the papers of his brother, Edward Bebb of Cilwinllan, I have seen

the names of the "Temperance-men" and the "Teetotalers" for that year. –W.A. Bebb

[39] *Ystyllen hysbysu* [pub sign]; literally, "informing plank."

[40] *Adar brithion;* shady characters.

[41] David Owen (1795-1866), itinerant preacher, editor, writer; by turns, Baptist, Independent and Anglican – as distinct from David Owen/ Dewi Wyn of Eifion (See note 24 above.)

[42] *Cystal iddo roi'r ffidil yn y to*; literally, "He might as well put the fiddle in the roof."

[43] The Presbyterian Church of Wales (*Yr Hen Gorff* [The Old Body]) comprises the Calvinistic Methodists and is the largest Nonconformist denomination Wales. This proliferation of labels merely hints at the doctrinal disputes Wm. Bebb so plainly deplores.

[44] Gwallter Mechain is the bardic name for Walter Davies (1761-1849), who served as vicar of Monafon, Montgomeryshire, from 1807 to 1837. Thomas Price (bardic name, Carnhuanawc; 1787-1848) served as a curate and vicar at various parishes in Breconshire. (See note 1 above).

[45] A reference, perhaps, to the impetuous young John Evans, of Waunfawr, Gwynedd, (1770-1799) who left Wales in a futile search for "The Welsh Indians of Madoc's race."

[46] *Breuddwyd gwrach*; wishful thinking.

[47] *Mawrth a ladd, Ebrill a fling.*

[48] *Eira call yn disgwyl y llall.* Compare with "*eira mân, eira mawr*" ["a fine snow, a heavy snowfall"].

[49] See note 19 above.

[50] *Clindarddarch* [sic] *drain dan grochan*; [first word should read *clindarddach*]. Literally, "the crackling of thorns under a cauldron." Cf., Ecclesiastes 7:6–"For as the crackling of thorns under a pot, so is the laughter of the fool: this is also vanity."

[51] A stereotypical image of Welsh bucolic innocence.

[52] *Gorau celwydd, celwydd golau.*

[53] Namely, "S.R." and his younger brother. –W.A. Bebb. (See note 6 above.)

[54] It's the time of the Vernal Equinox.

[55] Absinthe, a very bitter spirit that also serves as an analgesic.

56 John 5:39–"Search the scriptures; for in them ye think ye have eternal life: and they are they which testify of me."

57 Jeremiah 10:25–"Pour out thy fury upon the heathen that know thee not, and upon the families that call not thy name: for they have eaten up Jacob, and devoured him, and consumed him, and have made his habitation desolate."

58 Ephesians 4:29–"Let no corrupt communication proceed out of your mouth, but that which is good to the use of edifying, that it may minister grace unto the hearers."

59 Joshua 24:25–"So Joshua made a covenant with the people that day, and set them a statute and an ordinance in Shechem."

60 Exodus 20:6–"Remember the sabbath day, to keep it holy."

61 Colossians 3:22–"Servants, obey in all things your masters according to the flesh; not with eyeservice, as menpleasers, but in singleness of heart, fearing God:"

62 Ecclesiastes 11:9–"Rejoice, O young man, in thy youth; and let thy heart cheer thee in the days of thy youth, and walk in the ways of thine heart, and in the sight of thine eyes: but know thou that for all these things God will bring thee into judgment."

63 Genesis 34:1,2–"And Dinah the daughter of Leah, which she bare unto Jacob, went out to see the daughters of the land. And when Shechem the son of Hamor the Hivite, prince of the country, saw her, he took her, and lay with her, and defiled her."

64 Job 24:15–"The eye also of the adulterer waiteth for the twilight, saying, No eye shall see me: and disguiseth his face."

65 Proverbs 7:7-9–"And behold among the simple ones, I discerned among the youths, a young man devoid of understanding. Passing through the street near her corner; and he went the way to her house. In the twilight, in the evening, in the black and dark night:"

66 "Night courting, or 'bundling,' or courting on the bed was a widespread custom right across Europe in the Middle Ages. ... When the Education Commissioners of 1847 reported on the practice as evidence of unchastity and a frequent cause of illegitimacy, there was an indignant rebuttal from the *Cymry Cymraeg* [the Welsh-speaking Welsh]. ... It was also argued that country folk worked such long hours and had so little privacy that the only time they could do their courting was in this manner during the night, but that should not

A Welsh Hundred

be taken as an irretrievable loss of innocence." [from *Living in Rural Wales*, Noragh Jones (Gomer Press, 1993), p. 235]. (See note 28 above.)

[67] Pslam 101:6,7–"Mine eyes will be upon the faithful of the land, that they may dwell with me: he that walketh in a perfect way, he shall serve me. He that worketh deceit shall not dwell within my house: he that telleth lies shall not tarry in my sight."

[68] Compare this with a comment by S.R. in *Y Cronicl* ["The Chronicle"] (1857): "Of the people born in Llanbrynmair in the last 50 years, many more now live in America than in Llanbrynmair." –*W.A. Bebb*

[69] *Calan Mai*, or May Day, is a cross-quarter day that traditionally signifies the first day of summer. According to ancient Celtic calendar customs it was celebrated with the bonfire festival known as *Beltane* [*tân* being Welsh for "fire"].

[70] *Prif gantorion*; literally, "the principal singers."

[71] Namely, the oldest brother of the father of Mr. J.M. Howell of Aberdovey – that good Welshman who is such a generous President of the *Urdd* [*Gobaith Cymru*; i.e., the "Welsh Youth League"] today. William Howell was a boy of uncommon talent, and he died in 1826 at the age of 22. He left behind him several small books in splendid shorthand; and from the contents of some of them was compiled the *Monument to Methodism*, a volume of sermons published in 1884 – after S.R., now quite old, had transposed them into longhand (if I can call it such). –*W.A. Bebb*

[72] The Welsh *eisteddfod* is a time-honored competition for the bardic arts of poetry and music.

[73] *Minnau'n cloffi rhwng dau feddwl*; literally, "I am lame between two thoughts."

[74] The name of the Elias residence.

[75] Welsh spelling of the name of the Prophet Elijah.

[76] Midsummer's Day, the summer solstice.

[77] Hebrews 13:7–"Remember them which have the rule over you, who have spoken unto you the word of God: whose faith follow, considering the end of their conversation."

[78] Namely, the father of the bard Wmffre [Humphrey] Davies, who published a small booklet of poetry titled "Songs of Trefowen" in

Machynlleth in 1878. –*W.A. Bebb* [Dafis' nickname is of obscure origin; perhaps related to *cythraul, cythrol*, i.e., "the devil, the rascal."]

79 Independent Order of Rechabites, founded in 1835. (Cf. Jeremiah 35:8– "Thus we have obeyed the voice of Jonadab the son of Rechab our father in all that he hath charged us, to drink no wine all our days, we, our wives, our sons, nor our daughters.").

80 Is there not, perhaps, an implicit boast in Wm. Bebb's resort to three different languages within a single page of the original text? Welsh cosmopolitanism on display!

81 Enid [sister-in-law to W. Ambrose Bebb] brought this letter to my attention. –*W.A. Bebb*

82 *Y dref yn ddu gan ddieithriaid*; literally, "The town is black with strangers."

83 The first week of August is the beginning of autumn, according to rural tradition. This is the time when the ancient Celtic harvest festival of *Lughnasa* was celebrated.

84 *Y dydd bellach yn tynnu'i ben ato*; literally, the day is now drawing its head in.

85 Scythes for mowing hay; sickles for reaping grain.

86 William Bebb (1802-1873); said to be the first European born west of the Great Miami River in Butler County, Ohio; served as Governor of Ohio, 1846-1849, and later served as a pensions office examiner in the Lincoln administration.

87 S.R. was a cousin of his, on account of his mother and S.R.'s father being sister and brother. There was a correspondence between him and S.R. for years; and in a letter of July 1836, this sentence appears [in English]: "*I expect to see my cousin Sam Roberts in this country* (America) *next season*" – 21 years before S.R. did indeed emigrate. –*W.A. Bebb* (See note 6 above.)

88 Sir Robert Peel served as Home Secretary when the Metropolitan Police Act was passed in 1828. Soon thereafter, members of the London constabulary began to be referred to as "Bobbies." Since its institution in 1814, the Irish constabulary has similarly been referred to as "Peelers." Initially a protectionist, Sir Robert supported the Corn Duty; he later argued for its repeal.

89 Hot milk, curdled with wine or ale, sweetened and spiced.

90 The New Testament.

A Welsh Hundred

91 *"Diogyn"* [which can be translated not only as "receptacle for rush candles" but also as "sluggard; useless lazybones"] is the name for it in [the region of] Cyfeilog, from Cilwinllan to Cwmcarnedd Uchaf. It wasn't so "useless" in its heyday. –*W.A. Bebb*

92 Old New Year's Day. *Calan Gaeaf* [literally, "first day of Winter-month"] roughly coincides with the ancient Celtic festival of *Samhain*, the pagan prototype for Hallowe'en and All Soul's Day, which marked the onset of winter. *Samhain*, together with the aforementioned harvest festival of *Lughnasa*, the February festival of *Imbolc* and the May Day *Beltane* celebration, constitute the "cross-quarter days" of ancient calendar reckoning.

93 Presumably, a reference to the annual *Eisteddfod* literary competitions, at which a *Chairing* of the Bard recognizes the winning composition written in accordance with Welsh "strict meters" and a *Crowning* of the Bard honors the winning composition in Welsh free verse. The first and still the only chair comprehending Welsh studies at an English university is the Jesus Professorship of Celtic, founded at Jesus College, Oxford, in 1877.

94 Apparently, a reference to the letter writer's "frugal" habit of writing between the lines in ink of a different color.

95 This passage in English.

96 Namely, S.R. –*W.A. Bebb*

97 *Buost brin dy fraster, a bras dy brinder.*

1940:
Gleanings from a Diary

by
W. Ambrose Bebb

translated by
Marc K. Stengel
2008

originally published by
Wren Books
Llandebie, Carmarthenshire, Wales
February 1941

About the Book

[original publisher's note from the first (Welsh) edition]

Here's a book that will stun readers with its brilliance. We predict, in all good faith, that this small volume will set a world-record for sales of a Welsh book. As one expects from Mr. Bebb, he speaks without mincing words[1] – about his friends, about his own family, about the principal topics of the day, about politics. In reading this book, we re-live the fateful days of 1940. We move breathlessly[2] from scene to scene. It's a work pregnant with meaning and eloquence, yet simple and direct enough for a child to understand. A *tour de force* from a genuine artist.

Author's Dedication

For the Twins:
Hywel and Mererid

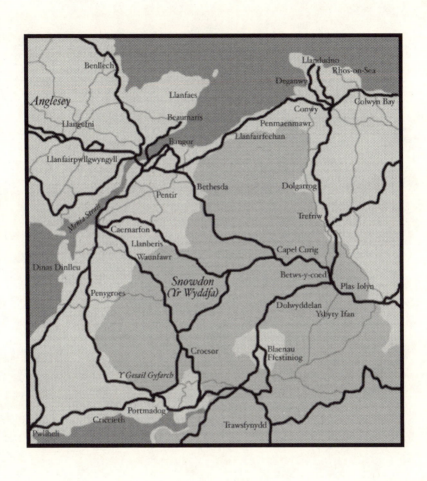

Map for 1940: Gleanings from a Diary

Preface

I long to share the blame for this book with its editors.[3] The idea for it belongs to them. I was contacted in September, while preoccupied with the harvest and without the least thought of tackling another literary project. Would I consider it? To some extent perhaps, I said. Later, I regretted that decision; and I wrote them to say so. "There's been *one* diary already.[4] Isn't that enough? That one was legitimate and had bubbled forth freely as a natural consequence of a single, unified experience during a critical fortnight in history. Yes, indeed – it simply gushed from the heart. But what now would be the purpose of another diary? Wouldn't it represent, perhaps, a mere shadow of my former attempt? "Only once in a lifetime does one climb a mountain of myrrh and a hill of frankincense," I protested.

"Only once – there is no second act!

"And besides, there would be no obvious connection between any new diary and my earlier one. The earlier book was a collection of similar, uninterrupted events experienced over a fortnight. But a year? Worse yet, the year hadn't exactly flowed along – shall I say – spontaneously."

My argument was unanswerable.

But the holidays came – and with them, leisure time. I leafed through the pages of my diary, and what I saw did indeed seem to come together as potential material for a book! A word to the Editors: I'd write up my diary for them after all. On Christmas Day, the terse telegram arrived: "Splendid! Immediately!"

Then, disillusionment struck. So I simply took it day by day; and behold the result: Gleanings from a diary that hadn't originally been written for anyone's eyes but my own. Tidy enough in private, I suppose; but in public, a mess!

W. Ambrose Bebb
Yr Hen Galan, 1941[5]

1940:
Gleanings from a Diary

THE FIRST CHAPTER

JANUARY 1ST: So here once again is the beginning of another diary. Why? I don't properly know myself, and I'm not sure there will be any real value in it. That's why I stopped keeping one last year. Free time was scarce enough just then; and I didn't have much more to record in a diary than discussions of work – my movements from classroom to classroom, for example, and from committee to committee or from City Council sessions to public meetings. That's all there was; that plus an occasional stint of writing – about Brittany, about the History of Wales and so forth.

I'm afraid it will be much the same again this year, with more work, less leisure time and more hardships – on account of the war. Yes, war. It's been with us for four months now; and it promises to continue for months more yet at the very least, but perhaps for more than a year. I was in France during the last fortnight of peace – if indeed one could call it peace; and I saw something of how the quiet life of Brittany was affected by the prospect of war. Later on, I saw how war extended its shadow over Wales, with thousands of refugees arriving in Caernarfonshire in the north and thousands more spreading out all across Wales. Their rhetoric was inflamed, and their mood was dejected. They were grimed with filth and stunned with disbelief. I also saw the havoc war was wreaking upon other aspects of our national life – the schisms of broken friendship,[6] for example; and the grousing about England's own culpability for escalating the conflict, whereas others contended it was all Germany's fault. I don't agree with the one opinion or the other. Certainly, England is no more sinless in the matter than France, by a wide margin. Nor does Germany deserve to be painted entirely black, either. Just the same, it's a fact that Germany has struck first, and there can be no denying that Germany has been scheming against and molesting the countries surrounding her for years. All because of the injustice of Versailles? You don't expect me to believe that, surely! It was the same in 1914…in 1911… in 1870…the same in 1814[7]…the same in the days of Frederick the Great. War is Germany's national industry. And war is the enemy of Civilization. Is it fair to attribute such capacity for evil to a *single* people exclusively? Prussia is the home of this evil – and Europe has allowed it to spread unchecked throughout Germany. The German aristocracy understood quite well what was happening – Goethe most of all, along with Heinrich Heine. Goethe spoke the truth when he observed that Germany's opportunity, her wealth, her civilization and, yes, even her peace were dependent upon the variety of cultures that constituted her component states.[8] The peace and tranquility of Germany's neighbors, and indeed of all Europe, were equally dependent upon this diversity. On second thought: Might not the same argument be adapted to conditions in England…as well as in France? It's a perfect fit! Especially as concerns Wales – and Brittany too. I can't imagine anything more *à propos*. Just the same, there's a difference between England and Prussia, between Prussia and France.

Let's leave it at that for a while – while things remain quiet, at least. We'll encounter plenty enough trouble in due course. In the meantime, I'll just see the holidays through in the company of Alphonse Daudet, Anatole le Braz, Emile Souvestre, Péguy and so forth.[9]

Luned[10] went off this morning to Llangadfan, where she's from; and she took the twins – Hywel and Mererid – with her. It'll do them good. It's a cold, icy morning. They'll get to see the countryside – the people of the countyside and its villages and its hearth-fires. They'll get to see a river flowing between its banks, ice on both a pool of water and a lake, and a layer of snow on the ground. Those little ones! For them, it'll be like spending time with the *Tylwyth Teg*.[11] It's dry and cold, with hard freezes every night; but the sun blazes in the sky every day. They'll get to be outside from dawn till dusk. And Luned will get a bit of respite from her onerous duties here – monotonous chores each and every day. I myself am staying home with Lowri, little Dewi – just one year, four months old – and our house girl. And Dic! He's been here since September – from London. He didn't know a word of Welsh when he arrived, and I was a bit concerned. I'm happy to say I needn't have been. He's learned Welsh quickly – on the run, as it were. By the end of the month, he was understanding everything. Now, he speaks quite well and even calls himself a Welshman!

JANUARY 9TH: The holidays come to an end, and it's back to the old routine! I get back to work in earnest – four lectures in the morning, two with the boys, two with the girls. And one more in late afternoon.

Luned's just back from Llangadfan, and the twins are now seasoned vets after their fortnight of trudging about the countryside. There's even a bit of Montgomeryshire accent in their speech. *"Neno'r ted*"!¹² The house is full once again – of unreserved congeniality; of incessant merriment; of noise, both pleasant and grating. What's wrong with that? It's just the face of a new year countenancing its future.

JANUARY THE 15TH: A letter from one of my old students: It deserves a rather unexpected "A." I read it through – simultaneously amusing and disturbing. It's in English, even though he knows a bit of Welsh. I blush with guilt when I come across one of his first sentences:

"I have often thought it would be a treat of a rare nature to meet you again, and talk with you – or rather listen to you talking." He of all people! He continues: *"I am in the Air Force…resplendent in blue grey, with delightfully bright buttons…have been since three weeks before Christmas. Early on it was novel, and strangely attractive…But the polish has worn off. I am getting restive. I want to kick, but here I dare not do so…I joined because I had to. There was no hope of a teaching post when war broke out. I was a big burden at home… there was no patriotism or heroism about it. I volunteered as a pilot (very selfishly I admit) believing that such a death would be far more glorious than the life I had lived so far. (I have always felt a romantic admiration for people who do a big thing and die)…But I hate it.*

"I am going astray. What I really want to say is that I am somehow ashamed of myself. I should have become a conscientious objector, but for two things. (a) The war issue was far from clear cut. There was no doubt about its Imperialistic nature. There was no doubt about profiteering. But there was also no doubt about the horror of Nazi-ism.

"(b) I had no desire to be linked with most of the C.O.s[13] *I heard about. No more conscience than the moon.*

"On the whole, I thought it better to die – so I volunteered as a pilot – not to kill, but to die. That was my honest intention. Now here I am as ordinary as they make them. A greater pawn than ever I shall be, or have been. I hate myself

for putting myself here, where I don't count for a brass farthing…I have only learnt one thing – that men are simple fools. I feel a traitor to all that is good.

"*I have been living in England (near London) for nearly two months now. I find it very different from my old life. I am getting near one of my confessions. The English are very different from the Welsh. Very, very different. I like the English more than the Welsh. (I had always imagined myself to be English!) I believe that what I regard as the better side of me, the romantic, impracticable, idealist, mountain-goat side, is the Welsh in me. But physically I am English – that is, the materialist side of me. I hate myself because it seems inevitable that while the English side will always be on top and come first, the Welsh Spirit will always be present to witness the treachery – and to accuse. In this letter the Welshman accuses the Englishman. There seems no hope that it will ever be different. I like living here very much. I like London. I enjoy eating in cafes with crowds. Going to cinemas and variety shows. But what I really want is in Wales. In Cwmbychan. Have you been there, Mr. Bebb? – the valley between Llanbedr and Trawsfynydd. And that is what you know to be true also. Therefore I have this confession. You are right. I am wrong. But I shall not change. Hence I can only say that life is mad, and nothing really matters – so why not eat, drink and be merry?*

"*It is only in the vague, unreal, dreamy world of thought that there seems to be sense and justice. But that world does not exist. The life we live, working, sleeping, eating and wasting time 'is a pig.' I feel that I cannot be bothered to live or to die. Certainly not to think. Nobody wants us to think, anyway. I become the enemy of society when I think. What a life!*"

I have quoted enough – perhaps a quarter of his letter. I know his anguish well enough. I'll write him back as soon as I can – all that wounded pride, the trampled independence. How can I not like him?

JANUARY 18TH: I've received a copy of *Ouest–Informations* [West–News], a small paper of some eight pages published by the National Party of Brittany. Published in Amsterdam! That's where Debauvais is –

and Mordrel, too, most likely.[14] How did they escape? When I saw them in Brittany at the end of last August, they were intending to join the army at once, "since there would be no war." And now they've escaped – from the army? – well, certainly from French soil. Who wouldn't admire their *presumption* at least? They provide a bit of news about Brittany, too – that's a treat. But now they're exiles; and I feel truly sorry for them.

JANUARY 26TH: Two hours lecturing about the decline of the Middle Ages and the approach of the Renaissance. How disagreeable! I read a lot from time to time about both periods; but I've not come across anything delightful about the Renaissance. The book by Burckhardt[15] is undoubtedly a significant and detailed work, and by many accounts the authoritative study. But he holds certain suppositions that are surely untrue: for example, he overemphasizes the asceticism of the Middle Ages; and he vigorously contends that men of that time weren't *the least bit* curious about themselves or the world around them. All these assertions can be rebutted, and Johan Nordström does so splendidly in his *Moyen-Age et Renaissance*.[16] O! one could scarcely wish for a more thorough book – or books, actually – than Nordström's for the way he deals so painstakingly with these two important eras.

• • • • •

For some three weeks after this entry, there has been simply nothing to record except for the fact that I'm buried in work day in, day out – from evening to evening as well, since I'm occupied almost every night producing a Welsh play at the College: *Modur y Siopwr* [The Shopkeeper's Car]. It's a light-hearted drama and easy to stage. We performed it the afternoon and evening of Saturday, the 17th of February – to the satisfaction of the audience, I believe; and to the playwright's satisfaction "more than anyone else's," he himself admitted!

He also said he'd seen the play performed four times previously, but three of our actors – Mari, William and Sarah – surpassed the actors playing their roles in the earlier productions. Whether this was true or not, I don't know. They're his words! As for myself, I'm very proud of *all* the actors for their spirited dedication to this project, even while up to their ears in college work. I'm thankful, just the same, to come to the end of this particular obligation, which stole so much of my time – to say nothing of the intractably cold conditions in our practice hall. It gets me to thinking about the soldiers in their camps – especially the Finns in their truly glorious battle. Imagine that small nation defying Stalin's monster empire – it should serve as an inspiration to *every* small nation.[17] David and Goliath all over again – except this time more splendid. It's the only magnificent act performed in this war, and this small nation has performed it. To the Finns! – heroes of the ice and snow… "all clad in their white smocks…"

FEBRUARY 19TH: One heck of a busy day. I lecture all morning, head out to the Glanadda School in the afternoon to listen to the boys [i.e., Bebb's students] giving history lessons to the children; then attend the Safety Committee after tea. At about 6:30, I address the "Spectators," one of the University's student societies, on the subject of Brittany. What with some discussion afterwards, it's already nine o'clock. In addition, I received today the first copy of my book, "*Dydd-lyfr Pythefnos, neu Y Dawns Angau.*" It has been at press for quite some time. It looks pretty good, as such things go – but it seems particularly fragile. In a quick scan, I catch a few minor errors – to be expected, I guess, since I was only provided a single proof-sheet. Price is 1/3 – extremely reasonable.[18] On the whole, I'm happy and quite pleased with it. Admittedly, it won't be of much interest to a lot of folks, because a knowledge of Brittany is essential for enjoying it properly. Luned read it tonight

A Welsh Hundred

while I was down at the College lecturing our students about the International Situation. It gave her – or so she says! – an excellent taste of the country.

FEBRUARY 24TH: I'm at the College by nine, and I lecture till midday. This afternoon, the Annual Conference of the National Party takes place in Caernarfon; it will be the first one I've ever missed since the party's founding. An astonishing thing, really – and, truly, a bitter pill.[19] A clear case of separating the inseparable – while "England profits from our dissension." The Party holds one viewpoint; I hold another. I've long maintained – since well before the outbreak of this war – that a united Germany (no matter whether it be Hitler's or William II's or Bismarck's Germany, so similar are they all) is a threat to European Peace. And though I have little sympathy with England, and none at all with her attempt to hold herself blameless, I do believe that a German victory would represent the utmost misfortune, even for us in Wales. It would be far better with me if Wales were free to choose her own side. This would be an ideal circumstance – if, that is, our pluck were even two-thirds as spirited as that of the Finns. But there's no such choice, and what a shame. Ah! If only the Party could keep the majority of Welsh boys out of the army. I beg you – this ineffectual negativism is just so unprofitable. Let this cup pass by![20] Let it *gallop* by!

FEBRUARY 29TH:[21] I awaken today – as I do almost every day – with little Dewi walking across the bedroom, standing still beside me for a minute till he puts his little, blond head down on my cheek and calls out, "Da-Da!" What more gentle wake-up call could anyone desire? What better sort of world could there possibly be to awaken to? What a dear, little, delightful creature he is.... Outside, I hear delightful sounds of another sort: birds of spring cheerfully weaving their web of early-morning song under a dawning sky. It's turning out to be a splendid day – indeed, a perfect day. A blue firmament, a laughing sun, warmth; ribbons of stone sparkling through the white snow on the mountainsides; sunny skies. And it's all filled with the sound of birds, dressed in flashing colors, chanting the spirit of joy…all the day long. I sit outside for what seems like ages and let the weight of all this beauty descend upon me and sink into me, and I listen to the voice of creation in all its unflustered calm. A day to remember, to keep alive in the memory against the onset of stormy weather. O, what a heavenly day!

The Second Chapter

March the 5th: A letter from another of last year's students – and it makes a great companion piece to the previous one. He's a rank Englishman, but a thoughtful and personable one at that. Not as much of a rebel as the other chap. He himself is in the army. I'll quote a bit of what he writes:

"*What cheer your letter, with all its memories of Bangor, brought. I have been in the army since December 1st. They have not been months of happiness – it's foolish to pretend – but the experience has not been entirely valueless. I have met so many different types of people – but nearly all have had to work for their living, some who have been born (almost literally) and have lived, in the factory. I can find few people with whom I can discuss ideas (So different from Bangor)… I can't pretend that I am not frequently irritated by the company I have to keep, and that I often long to flee from it all into some serene atmosphere where I could be peaceful and happy with just my own friends… But – c'est la guerre – and things have to be faced.*

"*I am sure that I should have been happier had I registered as a C.O. I seem to have abandoned all I ever believed in. And, as things have turned out my local Education Authority has not, as it stated it would, made up my salary. Consequently, I am unable to help at home either. I knew of this exactly a week before I was due to report at the camp. I could not make up my mind what to do. Even by the last day I had not reached a decision. I suppose that in the end I didn't decide anything, but drifted helplessly along. I have regretted it bitterly since. This heavy sense of utter futility is the price I have to pay. I haven't even the consolation now of knowing that I am helping the family… How I should love to have one of those Thursday night meetings again, when you used to address us on International*

Affairs… Thank you again for your letter. It did more for me than you can imagine…."

Another soul in turmoil. These boys are really suffering, aren't they? They're considered rebels. But aren't flashes of truth showering off their consciences like sparks off an anvil? He'll get his next letter from me before long.

MARCH 7TH: In *y Faner*,[22] there's a rather lengthy review by Saunders Lewis of my book *Cyfnod y Tuduriaid* [*Age of the Tudors*[23]]. Extremely interesting, and a special treat to read. It's very complimentary – a bit too complimentary in fact, even as it needles me a little for some of my notions…subtly, but unmistakably. I wonder if he's correct to esteem the latter part of the book over the former? It's the more comprehensive portion, admittedly; tighter and more carefully structured – on account of my having to eliminate and prune so much material from the earlier sections.[24] He's probably right.

MARCH 11TH: This school term is drawing to a close; and since the boys and girls in their second year are doing their in-service training in Anglesey and Caernarfonshire, we teachers are heading out after them to observe – to weigh and measure them, so to speak! Today, I head to Llandudno. On the train, two boys in their first year are my fellow-travelers. The one is from Rhos, the other from Colwyn Bay; both are on their way to London to request an extension of their College term. Will they succeed? "Hardly likely,"[25] as they say in Caernarfonshire. They look passive – but not very contented. Theirs is the passivity of a tormented slave. I part company with them at Llandudno Junction and wish them all the best – feeling half-guilty at the same time. What small, helpless creatures. We've already lost two or three of them so far this term. From now until summer, we'll lose more – and more yet from summer to September. It will create both a rift and a hole, a schism and emptiness, in the life of the College. And a sense of loss and disappointment. Just thinking about it is painful.

I visit two schools. The boys are trying their level best, and the occasional one is truly brilliant. I look around me – prospects for the Welsh language, *Cymraeg*, are so very gloomy. She – Welsh, that is – has traveled all the way to London in search of a new lease on life! What are her chances? All other school subjects have made the same trip – and they've each caught the ears of the education authorities. But poor *Cymraeg*! How much bureaucratic support and official encouragement will our Welsh-language teachers get?

I turn back for home, and after tea I attend the Electrical Power Committee meeting. Then, I finish the day in style with a book by the Canon [Roger Bradshaigh] Lloyd – *The Golden Middle Age*. Most satisfactory.

MARCH 14TH: Two hours of lecturing, both of them in Welsh. How easy and agreeable. Back home, I read sad news about the war in Finland. It concerns yesterday and today, and it seems frightfully alarming and disastrous. For three months and more by all accounts, the Finns were heroes, performing almost miraculous feats of valor. They defied blackest oppression and cruel arrogance. They stared into the muzzles of gun-barrels; faced innumerable troops and regiments; and harvested thousands of the enemy upon their snowy proscenium. Then – the abrupt *finale*! Their territory, which had been sanctified by the blood of its slain defenders – lost. Their fortresses, their rocky redoubts – all lost. It seems so unbelievable. How to explain it? Surely not by any sort of feebleness or lack of resolve on the Finns' part. All is not yet revealed, of course. Did they fight in vain? Well, greatness is never in vain — nor is valor, nor any noble, decent gesture. Their struggle will live on in the mind, in the memory, in the tales and the songs of their nation — and in those of all humankind. Finland Forever!

MARCH 19TH: I visit the schools of Llandudno throughout the day; and the Supervisors are there too, a rather important trinity of them in fact. Our boys are already aware of them, so they're not too anxious. They keep their heads — and their balance. All their worries are now at an end. They laugh everything off. They share their experiences with one another, faces beaming with smiles. The holidays are on their way.

The big news of the day concerns the meeting between Hitler and Mussolini at Brenner Pass. The papers are full of conjectures and predictions. What can these noisy, blinkered experts possibly know?

Another issue of *Ouest-Informations* arrives. There's a fairly long article by Debauvais — who's still in Amsterdam — in which he castigates France. With good reason. Just look at the news: Lainé,[26] so ready to smile when I saw him last August, has been sentenced to jail. He didn't manage to escape, then. I know he'll be wearing a sunny smile as he faces jail yet again. This, he believes, is how Brittany will be roused — through the suffering of the Strong the Weak will be saved. It's going to be four years of jail for Joseph Marie Colin as well. "Hard-headed Bretons" is one of their favorite self-descriptions — and it's true. What a storehouse full of dedication they have! More news — France has shut down *Ker Vreiz* (*Tŷ Llydaw*),[27] a sort of home away from home that the Bretons have maintained in Paris. And the government has also banished publication of the periodical *Sav*.[28] Worst of all, in the city of Rennes, they have burned Breton books, dictionaries and traditional Breton songs; and in Quimper, part of the Museum was set on fire. Have the French authorities lost their bloody minds? It's nothing but savage, cruel madness – entirely unpardonable. There will be vengeance to pay for this.

There's other news, of a somewhat different sort, concerning the deaths of three quite prominent Bretons: the bard Charles Rolland; the arch-authority on Breton pre-history, Zacharie Le Rouzic; and the bard and literary giant Dr. [C.A.] Picquenard. I knew all three quite well, especially the first two. Rolland was the archetypal bard of the peasantry and common folk, a wild and talented genius. And Rouzic, himself of peasant stock, strode to real distinction by way of scholarship. What a great loss for Brittany – to say nothing of my own sense of grief and torment.

MARCH 25TH: Easter Monday. And not only that: it's a truly splendid day, both sunny and warm. I spend the entire morning outside on the stoop, reading the papers – two or three of them from France.

After dinner, we all make our way towards Llanbabo – and so as not to sin against the good people there, we call it by the name they prefer: Deiniolen.[29] We go to Miss Mai Roberts' home. Luned stays in the house with Mai and her mother. The children and I head for the bank of the stream at the back of the house – it's called *Caled-ffrwd* [Hard-rushing-torrent]. We play about and shout at one another; hop along the stream's large stones; and play tag. We sit, spending refreshing moments just drinking-in the plash of the brook, the peace of its babbling waters. Here in our own special haven we're oblivious to world and town. It's so comfortably calm! They call us back to the house, and we enjoy a rustic, cozy teatime. Our strength restored, the children and I leave the crowded houseful behind again and climb up the rough hills and craggy rocks towards the highest crests, which overlook Llanberis Lake. Around towards the left, tumps of hills climb onto each others' backs, with *Yr Wyddfa* [Mount Snowdon] towering above them. It sits there imperturbable amidst its surroundings, unchanging, contented, sun-washed. To the right, relatively charmless towns and houses blanket the hillsides and extend up and down their slopes right to the edge of a basin of gorgeous countryside through which one, maybe two rivers shimmer jewel-like under the hazy sky. How far all this is from the clamor of the world! Everything we've left behind is just a whisper now....

"Never will all of earth's tumults disrupt heaven's calm...Nor will the bustle of man and his world disturb its tranquility...We are forever fleeing from our own foolish fretting"![30]

An escape from affliction; a fort on a hill; a refuge for Welshmen's thoughts. What a remarkable interlude of just a few splendid moments gleaned from such tempestuous days as these. We climb down and leave – already nostalgic for the afternoon that has by now disappeared at a swift clip. But it has left behind memories and views of pure enchantment. On the way back home, the children holler and shout about the myriad wonders encountered this day. Dewi can hardly bring himself to doze in my lap, what with all the fun he had during those few magical hours. But they – those hours – will settle under his eyelids tonight and regale him again with their secrets as he sleeps in peace. He and Hywel and Mererid and Dic will be chattering all about them tomorrow – and for several days more, I suspect. Lowri is staying in Deiniolen for another week. Lucky her!

MARCH 31ST: Sunday – and I've promised to address some sort of men's association near Rhyl that calls itself a *"Progressive Group."*[31] I'm now repenting profoundly that I ever agreed; but I go just the same despite the inhospitable weather. My topic is *Wales, Her Joys and Her Sorrows*. I reach town totally discouraged – I hate Rhyl, I think, more than any other town in Wales. I stand before Mostyn Café, then I step in. It's a fairly large room, and about 40 people are there – both men and women, and three soldiers. Moreover they're all Socialists, if they really know what that means. I speak for 20 minutes – in vain, as the discussion following my comments makes clear. What is Wales to these scabs? O, the small, small heart that beats within the International Socialist! They see the evils of capitalism – in England. They bewail injustice – *to the far ends of the earth*. But what about Wales, where these same evils are so rife? Not one word! They vomit their guts out prattling endlessly about reforms; but they close their eyes to the urgent need of reform right here in Wales. They bleat about a world of free nations, but Wales certainly isn't numbered amongst them. O, the hypocrisy!

April 3rd: I've been in a gloomy mood for days. And I've stayed in bed later than usual this morning. Luned brought *The Banner* up to the bedroom. She was very proud, having just read the review of *A Fortnight's Diary* by Saunders Lewis. She read it to me, and I hid the tears that escaped from under my eyelids when I heard the words, "A literary masterpiece…a splendid novel…a book to cherish, a true diary…that puts personal insights and anguish on display." Why shouldn't I weep? It wasn't the extent of the praise, the keenness of the criticism, that turned my eyes into fountains. Instead, it was the realization that it had all come from a friend who now considers me – yes, it must be said – unfaithful to the old dream, to the Party, to Wales. And yet, such magnanimous generosity! However, one might as well point out the sharp cunning of a sentence or two – the suggestion that I have another love besides Brittany, greater than Brittany – namely, France. Then, there's the lingering emphasis upon the words, "Does he perhaps identify with *their* ways now?" These have a sting in them.[32] As a result, my breast is filled with troubled joy. With joyful melancholy.

APRIL 5TH: For several days now, I'll be on holiday once again. And I intend if at all possible to read the complete works of the bards, from the time of Dafydd ap Gwilym right through to Tudur Aled. I chiefly want to discover what materials they themselves might have read and consulted, and so forth. I've already gleaned much from the work of Dafydd and his contemporaries; from Iolo Goch and his contemporaries; and from Guto'r Glyn and Ieuan Delwyn.[33] There are abundant references in their work to every sort of secular Romance. And it's fascinating to observe how these worldly preoccupations multiply. Nevertheless, weren't Welsh tastes in reading-matter as well as in oral, bardic traditions every bit as Roman Catholic as those evident in all the other literatures and tales and beliefs of the Middle Ages throughout Western Europe? Next, I change tack and put in a fair amount of time working in the garden – digging, tilling, weeding, turning soil, furrowing, planting, and sowing. I end the day with Owst and his examination of the Pulpit and Sermons of the Middle Ages.[34] Quite interesting.

APRIL 9TH: A crazy morning. The painter came by – what a disaster. Everything was absolutely helter-skelter. I was feeling angry, miserable, out-of-sorts, malicious. So I went out, thankful for the open air. Even that didn't work! Because I heard about Hitler's attack on Denmark and Norway. Is the great crisis really looming now – to be accompanied by some awful, horrible massacre?

APRIL THE 10TH: More details, and the rumors are verified; Denmark is already in Hitler's hands, and Norway is in peril. So tranquility and security have come to an end for these small nations. It's really quite sad. What good did it do them, placing all trust in their naïve, fickle, idealistic Democracies with such a fully armed neighbor right next door? Does this mean that the day of the small nation is now past? One certainly might think so. Small nations today need to face hard facts: Ours is a century of iron. Does it pay to lie so tidy, snug and pampered in your own small nest if that means closing your ears to the birds of prey screeching all about you? After all, in this world there is no arbiter between nations. There is no moral power sufficient to overwhelm the hosts of oppression. Our world simply lacks the legions of activists necessary for safeguarding the peace. Where have all of us in Europe been, lately? Are we not meticulously dismantling all of our essential institutions – and galloping madly, like stampeding cattle with tails in the air and no thought of turning back, towards the gates of perdition?

APRIL 11TH: More horrible news: hard fighting on the high seas off the coast of Norway, as well as aerial attacks and land assaults. Norway is being torn apart by dogs and ravens, and it will be the great loser. I think about a friend or two I have there, in Oslo – Somerfelt, who taught with me in Paris, is as industrious and unflagging as an ant; Maarstander is another, whom I saw only once or twice. What will be their fates now? Will they be forced to escape? To go back to their digs in Paris? Or might they come to Britain, to Wales? Somerfelt has been here once or twice before. I daydream about being able to meet him, to welcome him to Bangor. What nonsense!

APRIL 12TH: The painter's still here, and everything's still a mess. I try to keep an eye on Dewi's wild forays through the clutter, the buckets of paint, the ladders, the brushes and so forth. As for myself, I'm just puttering about when suddenly there's this loud cry – a monstrous shout, a dreadful shriek and tears raining down. Everything is pure commotion, and Dewi is running around holding both hands overhead. They're up to the wrists in green paint! Was it a cry of fear? Or of guilt? Either way, what follows is a lot of rubbing, scrubbing, lathering and washing. "That's it! Come here, you little devil, you." He's quiet now – for about two minutes. Then, he's back to his exploits. But this time, I'm his target. He pulls at my nose, my eyebrows, my hair. He stares into my eyes and puts his fingers into them, then tousles my hair. His two hands throttle my neck. Some improvement!

April 18th: The College re-opened two days ago. For a week, the first-year boys and girls go off to student-teach in schools. This time, the boys are in Anglesey – how delightful! So the day before yesterday, I got to travel across the island, and I enjoyed seeing the countryside come alive, in spite of the cold. In the fields, small lambs pranced about; and cattle were grazing enthusiastically, even breathlessly, as if they'd never seen a green pasture before. The occasional farmer – an old man, every time! – was scattering seed on the furrowed face of his land. Then, yesterday, I was off in another direction, where I encountered a school principal who turned out to be this remarkably ancient old worm. He cast his shadow – a shadow of old age and despair, fatigue and disgust – over the entire school; and the Welsh language was wasting away under his blighted influence. Blessed heavens! How long must this go on?

Today, I'm off to three delightful schools – in Newborough, Dwyran and Brynsiencyn. Welsh is spoken here, as unselfconsciously as if at home by the fireside. The whole atmosphere is so lighthearted and animated and youthful in its Welshness. In Newborough, that venerable sense of initiative so hard to find elsewhere is fully *alive* in this school, and the children are developing splendidly by sinking their roots into their own native culture. What wonderful schools! It was a splendid day for me, as I dashed briskly from one school to another, then home afterwards. Tomorrow, I'll travel again to interesting schools in the middle of the shire. Two days later, however, it will be a very different situation altogether. As usual, I'll be rebuking the headmaster. And again, as usual, he'll suffer his rebuke like a small child – yet persist in his inveterate and ineffective ways. The rascal! If we had a perfect system, *he'd* have to be perfect too.

April 29th: Monday morning. Last night, the Church chose its deacons. My first news of the day is that I am one of the elect. It beggars belief! What to do? Accept? Refuse? How can I accept, since I am – dare I say it – so unworthy? Throughout the day, people's expressions of "congratulations" sound so empty – as parched as a raven's croak. So I'll refuse then? That's the only fair and decent thing to do. "It's an insult to the Church!" says this one, that one and the other behind my back. The minister comes over, and I tell him my situation. I promise to think it over.

April 30th: The boys and girls have finished their student-teaching. Now we're back under full sail with our College work. Four lectures this morning: History, Scripture and Welsh – two hours for the latter. At 5:30 in the afternoon, the fifth lecture: History once again; and we discuss an enjoyable but difficult topic, namely, "The Enlightened Despot of the 18th Century." Aren't the history books rather ambiguous and vague on this subject? They only scratch the surface, really. How often do they attempt to analyze the essential difference between the "Enlightened Despot" and any other despot – or king, for that matter? How were Frederick the Great, Catherine the Great, any more enlightened than, say, Louis the Great of France, Henry the IV of England and, yes, even Philip II of Spain? Wasn't so-called "enlightenment thought" frequently nothing more than an outright expression of anti-religious or anti-

Papist sentiment? And wasn't that simply the prevailing spiritual climate of the century? Vanity of vanities! You call Frederick the Great enlightened?...and Catherine the Great! This much about them *is* true at least: great was their greed! Joseph II of Austria was the best of the lot; but even his reputation, by all accounts, is spotty enough.

The Third Chapter

May the 2ⁿᵈ: All hail to you, Merry Month of May! This year more than ever – Hail, Hail to you! *"Pan ddel Mai…"*³⁵ Today, May has truly arrived. It's a genuine May Day indeed.³⁶ Birdsong, sunny warmth, beautiful surroundings; all of it's here – and the sun is ambling along amongst the trailing tatters of white clouds. There's an indistinct haze of green leaves and buds on the tree branches and hedgerows, and it's just hovering there between earth and sky. What an enchanting display of the skein of nature.

A light workload today; only two lectures. In the middle of the first one, a telegram arrives asking one of the boys to call home – before he heads out for the army tomorrow! He is one of those two fellows I traveled with while they were on their way to London hoping to obtain an extension for their College studies. Well, there's your answer! A stunned silence overtakes the classroom. It's the boy from Rhos; and he leaves immediately, with a feeling of emptiness trailing off after him. Yesterday, yet another one was gone. It was D.R. Jones, a member of the drama company and the only son of a quarryman from Bethesda. I gave him a copy of *A Fortnight's Diary*. He left my house, and tears secretly welled up in his eyes. He was heading out to France…then to Egypt, to Canaan³⁷…!

May the 9ᵗʰ: Two lectures – on the History of Wales in the days of Henry VIII. When the lectures are over, the students want to spend their mid-morning half-hour break discussing topics of the day – the war, its developments, its recent disappointments. Poor wretches; how young they are to be forced into the realization – as I am myself – that our lives are being controlled by dark forces. The awful news that Hitler has invaded Holland tortures them.

They question; cross-examine; answer; respond; despair; rejoice; hope and lose hope – all in the very same breath.

May the 10th: Bad news on the heels of bad news. The heck with it! I want to escape. It's half-term; so I have this afternoon, all day tomorrow (Saturday) and Sunday free to myself. It's a chance to head out into the countryside. I haven't been away from Bangor since I returned from France, just four hours before war exploded. I make my way to Tregaron, and Dic comes with me – so I can leave him in my brother's care at the farm, on account of the new addition to our family we're expecting any day now. His Welsh is already almost perfect – he'll be a proper Cardi[38] in no time! He's gotten a friend from Aberystwyth to haul us out there. Pretty convenient. We set out about one o'clock. As we leave Bangor, the clouds part and the sun re-appears – and it doesn't go back into hiding for the rest of the day. It wants to give us a perfect afternoon and blanket the countryside with a kaleidoscope of colors – every shade of green for the woods and the fields; soft yellow upon the myriad oaks; white and crimson on the copses and gardens; a haze of dark green and purple Lady's-smocks over the crags and uplands and sheep-walks. This little flower throws its color into the air like a sort of incense that kisses the ground without alighting upon it. At the summit of *Yr Wyddfa*, spotless, buoyant clouds resemble an immaculately white beard. Aberglaslyn Bridge just sits there calmly between a phantasm of yellow, budding leaves above and foaming, babbling waters below. And skirting the Vale of Maentwrog are abundant clusters of rhododendron, some in richest red, others mottled in red and purple. I rise from my seat and gaze, wide-eyed, to my right, to my left, backwards and forwards as magnificent Creation marches past in a steady stream of wonders that appear and disappear one after the other. We stop by Hafan house in Bow

Street, [Aberystwyth,] so I can call in on my old Professor – Gwynn Jones. Here he is, in the garden, wearing rather coarse homespun. He's smiling, but his face is wan – and it's not his usual jovial smile, either. He turns towards the house, very slowly. Sits. Looks for his collar. Finds his shirt and knots his tie…he seems particularly lethargic. He sits down again and speaks, listlessly. He's not sour or morose but curt, both in his breathing and in his choice of words. I *venture* to ask: is he working…writing? A cough. "No, not at all… not any more. I've written the last book I'll ever write." He draws a breath. I wonder why?

"No…people have no interest in common sense these days!"

Things will get better again in time, Mr. Jones.

"No…not any more…not at all…"

There's nothing to gain from pursuing this line of conversation. So I change the subject and start talking about Brittany, and Ireland! *Tir Na'n Og!*[39] At last, here's one of the old smiles casting a flicker of dawn's light upon his pallid face, while the faintest spark kindles his incomparable eyes into flame. He recalls his travels in Ireland; recalls receiving his Doctorate there, and meeting with Douglas Hyde and de Valera.[40] Nearly his old self again…the Gwynn we all knew…*my* Gwynn. Well, *almost*. And, as a result, my thoughts grow heavy as I take my leave. Maybe I'm feeling a little guilty as well? He, my old professor, does he too think I'm being unfaithful to the ideal…to the cause of Peace? It agonizes me! But we have to move on. I catch a glimpse of Aberystwyth – the College Tower, the fortress-like National Library, the sea. It's all interwoven into such a pleasant, half-magical atmosphere – if only because of so many personal connections of mine. Over to my friend's house next, where I listen to the news – such intoxicating madness. Then off again, to Tregaron. We reach the old homeplace before nine. Everyone's well; there are cheerful faces all round and a peat fire in the hearth. "My cup is full."[41]

I spend three full, enchanting days here – everything's so quiet and peaceful without a paper, without any news. I walk the fields; climb the uplands; follow sheep trails; cross over the fens via causeways and wooden bridges and dykes. I chat with my brother and the farm hands about the appearance and condition of the fields. We call them by their names as if they were living persons, each one with its special requirements and crop, each one's yield already stipulated. There'll be seed hay, fallow-field hay, pasture grass, potatoes, turnips, oats, barley and wheat – yes, the King of Corn himself[42]; wheat again for the first time in years. Time to welcome the exile back, this grain of ancient pedigree.

I am absolutely flourishing in the calm sensuality of life that surrounds me here; amidst such unremitting greenness, accompanied by the constant song of the cuckoos and birds of the fens; by the murmer of streams and brooks; the subtle sounds of cattle grazing and harrows disking; the ewes and lambs bleating absent-mindedly into the void. And everywhere, the small, frail, newly germinated ferns are unfurling their fiddleheads in the warmth of the sun.

MAY 13TH: I head back home – much too soon, of course. A thousand heartstrings have started to bind me to this place again. How bitter it is to pull up my roots from the very soil that still clings to them – all because I bothered to show my face around here one more time. There's nothing to do for such heartbreak but just let it bleed; and it does, profusely, all the way back – through the same beguiling splendor, mind, as on the way down.

Bangor once again, buzzing with all the meaningless commotion of city folk. There's disturbing news racing about – Holland has capitulated unconditionally. Where are my friends from Brittany now?

Debauvais, Mordrel? Did they manage to escape? Did they have a secret plan? Tonight, my soul is troubled. And it longs for the countryside.

MAY 16TH: I'm lecturing today. On the way to school, I make a hurried stop at the University Library. The vestibules are crowded with students weaving their way past one another. I hear a voice calling out and two footsteps coming up behind me. Another call, closer this time. Who is it? Madamoiselle Cariou, who's a French lecturer here. She looks agitated. "I want to see you," she declares. She's too insistent; I have to comply. "What the matter with…?"

"Come into my room. Just for a minute…half a minute, that's all." O, heavens. I follow her. Just as we reach the door she asks me, with startling directness,

"*Est-ce que vous avez une bombe?* ["Do you have a bomb?"]

"*Une bombe?…Pourquoi faire?*" ["A bomb? What on earth for?"]

"To destroy that trio of traitors on this campus…which is overrun with their kind. Three-quarters of my students are conscientious objectors. My own co-lecturer is an enemy of France."

She threw herself into the arms of a chair and gave way to bitter tears. Tears and words, spurting out together: "*A! Mon Dieu*, why did I ever come here?…why did I ever leave France?…to come to this place? *Mon Dieu, mon Dieu!* I'm alone…alone…so all *alone*. Everyone here is an enemy of France…except for you. You…are France's only friend…." These last words trailed off into wretched groans.

For heaven's sake; what a mess! What to do? Should I comfort her? How? Tell her that France will be all right – on the eve of invasion? By all means, there's nothing else for it. They're sugar-candy words, but they weave their web of magic and fantasy. Her tears dry; she rises from her chair – and I hurry off! I happen to be in complete sympathy with her, of course. But why can't she keep her composure?

A change of pace: I receive a card from someone I have absolutely no connection with, and this is all it says: "Dear Mr. Bebb: Just finished your Diary [*A Fortnight's Diary*]. The best book I've read in ages. Many thanks for writing it. Sincerely, Ll. Wyn Griffith." Things are looking up – for a moment anyway.

MAY THE 18TH: These days are most incompatible with the pleasantness of May. They are, instead, heartbreakingly sad, on account of the news out of Belgium and France. We're hearing about the occupations of Brussels, Malines, Louvain; about the tank assaults and the blitzkrieg invasions of country after country – now reaching into French territory itself. One moment, we're worried sick about all those people surrounded by fire and burning and heinous killing; the next moment, which is in fact the longer of the two, we're fretting over the way even the faintest echo of news about these killings has simply vanished from earshot. The air is heavy with fear, with dread, with horror. A great weight – a prodigious, oppressive weight – is bearing down upon the mind, the breast, the heart. Lecturing is becoming hard work – meaningless, unrewarding, uncongenial work. Reading is likewise unprofitable – pure foolishness. The hours I spend are *all* unpleasant, full of bad omens.

I had a strange experience listening to tonight's news. The most significant item had to do with Maréchal Pétain[43] being recalled from Spain. What an astonishing thing: Suddenly my dark misgivings come to an end, and a certain ease-of-mind, even satisfaction, takes their place. But – he's an 80-year-old man, isn't he? What can he possibly do at this grim hour? And after the politicians have made such a muddle of things? For it's the unprincipled, disreputable politicians who have paralyzed the life of the fairest, richest nation in Europe! They should bathe in their own vomit for that.

MAY THE 20TH: O! these sunny days! Sunlight – and blood, both of them soaking into the soil. Getting up in the morning is pleasant, a moment of communion with the earth as it too awakens. "The Fledgling Day" is a fair enough description of the animated calm and quiet intensity that distinguish these hours. They're full of virtue and vigor, which percolate into the mind and the breast, and from there into the spirit and the soul. More's the pity, then, that it all comes to shambles when I call to mind the killings and the atrocities befalling those places I know so well, places I love almost as dearly as my own doorstoop.

MAY 21ST: Four lectures in the morning, one in the evening. But they don't seem to give any meaning, as they once did, to the many hours of thought and work that go into composing them. Beyond the lecture hall, surrounding it, pervading it, is the thick, heavy shadow of war. I follow all the news I can in a state of daily – and intensifying – distress. People are asking one another about the meaning of this, that and the other thing. They crave the latest report but dread its arrival. Everyone appears dejected and broken-hearted. Everyone pays attention to every word and prediction. They doubt; they dread; they worry. They cringe, then they come undone.

MAY THE 22ND: People are stepping onto the thresholds of their houses and shouting from one doorway to the other. This is how they spread the news, truth and lies alike. "The news…it's a little better today." It looks like Pétain and Weygand have turned the tide with nothing more than a word from their lips. Let it be so! At the College, everyone is agitated, frantic to have just one word of hope, of encouragement. What did Gamelin do? How could such negligence take place? What will become of him? Most importantly of all, what can Weygand do now?[44]

May the 25th: Another ray of light – more so than yesterday anyway. There's much rejoicing in the air. Everyone greets you on the way to the College with the same question: "Any better news from France today?" There isn't even time to say, Good Morning. We're all one big, nervous brotherhood! How true is the news we get? More to the point, how long can we trust it to remain true? I couldn't tell you any more than a dead man could. "Let your ignorance be your hope," is all I can say. Even in the best of circumstances, uncertainty and inconstancy are the tokens of war. And this war is certainly no exception.

But we put everything behind us for the afternoon, so that Luned, Dewi and I can head out into the countryside – to Pentir. They visit a house – the home of that incomparable harpist Nansi Richards. As for myself, I take to the fields; and along some narrow trails, I lose myself in a child's admiration for the leafy hedgerows, the shapely woods, the meadow-flowers, the birdsong and the scents of ferns and grasses. A handsome wood, a field of hay – aren't these but two of Creation's masterpieces? I feel like I'm swimming – through life, through the air, through the very genius of this place. What pleasures can compare with the pleasure of common things – with the pleasure of the natural world's delicate little graces? Just being in their presence is joy and satisfaction in itself. There is nothing to compare with the delight of their appearance or with the charm that radiates out of them back into this world which positively teems with them. Here I am, so close to Bangor…and yet so far – so safe and so far, if only for a fleeting moment. Teatime is splendid – and then, setting a brave face, we make for home.

May 25th: Back to bad news. Calamitous news. Belgium and France are a massacre. I won't stand for it, because I know first-hand about the pluck and the passion of the sons of France. I can see her wheat fields and her vineyards, her charming cities and her splendid churches. I see, I see…what *don't* I see? My heart bleeds – literally bleeds – when I think about this hallowed ground being under the control of barbarians who are unable – nor will they *ever* be able – to appreciate the lovely, humane civilization that flourishes so elegantly there.

May 28th: After reaching the College a little before nine in the morning, I hear that the Prime Minister of France delivered a broadcast at eight. Why? What did he say? No one knows. I discover only later that he announced that the King of Belgium had commanded his army to surrender its arms. What gives?[45] I don't know what to think. It's all so confusing: Did he ignore the advice of his generals? Or was it sheer hopelessness? Perhaps all the killing terrified him? Or was it…who knows? But if the king stands aside, yet his army is determined to fight, won't there be more death and destruction than ever? Did he truly make…the best choice?

May 29th: King Leopold's behavior is the object of everyone's criticism – even though there's not a single living soul who knows what all his considerations were. People are completely losing their heads! "This is extraordinary," somebody says; "that's just unbelievable," says somebody else; and yet they have the nerve to criticize the one and only person who is in possession of all the facts. "He's not like his father, that's for sure." Who can say? Let patience run its course! I'm waiting for the facts first. Still though, I'm surprised he didn't warn his Government – or Weygand, at least – before deciding. Yet, if he had…?

May 30th: The situation is bleak – bleak as hell, though not irreparable I tell myself. So far, the machines[46] are in charge. But when *man's* hour comes at last – at that hour when powers of the spirit, of understanding, of the mind, of the will – whenever that time comes, I have no doubt that France will win. Already, there are hints that her political arrangements have improved. Pétain is in the government – at its summit. Then, too, there is Weygand. Now there can be no doubt that the government and the army will understand each other better. Such a shame. Does this sort of calamity have to happen before a Republic comes to its senses? How addle-brained; but better late than never, at least! Ach! Who's now better off after all the mistakes that've been made? Let's ask the slaughtered multitudes.

May 31st: I deliver a broadcast out of Bangor concerning a delightful topic: France and her People. I have a particularly good time of it, and I'm truly proud to have had this opportunity to pay homage to a France suffering such grievous, dreadful circumstances. With easy conscience, I can now return to my books and read – about the Renaissance in Italy, as it so happens. O! how I wish I had the power to prove to Italy that its truest, its best advantage lies in taking France's side. If Mussolini is the man I think he is, this realization should be as clear as day.

The Fourth Chapter

June the 3rd: In the morning, my Welsh-language students take their oral examinations. It's the most curious thing! Not even half of them are well enough prepared.

At about 4:30, I take Luned down to Craig Beuno Infirmary. A genuine Welsh infirmary, where our four others were all born as well. I stay a while…then hurry home and have tea. I relax in the garden for a bit and read; it's the nicest day we've had so far this year. Truly, a perfect summer's day.

I'm back at the infirmary by ten. I wait. One of the nurses comes down: "Congratulations! It's a boy. He's just fine…a strong one…" My anxiety comes to an end. I'm a little overwhelmed – that's the fifth one, three sons, two girls; all of them strong, healthy, flawless. Thank-you…*thank-you*! The doctor comes down shortly and confirms the news. He's a gentle man and quiet, thrifty in speech. We share some tea and have a little chat. He says, "What a splendid evening! I hope they'll be bombing Berlin tonight." There you have it: Giving birth… Waging death…!

June the 7th: I lecture till noon then go home through the fields; and the sun is splendidly hot. On my way, I read the copy of *Ouest-Informations* that arrived this morning. Debauvais and Mordrel are in Hungary! And they're proclaiming that France's time has come to an end. In a few days, she will have been completely defeated and overrun. They proclaim; they declare; they behave as if they're infallible. They have a radio service and everything…!

"*Allo! Allo Kenvroiz.*

"*Neventi vat da vruda!*

A Welsh Hundred

"Selavit holl: Radio Breiz a gas kelou d'eoch bem noz etre 20 eur ha 20/15." [47]

There's no way to convince them. What a capital farce they are! When I get back to the house, Dewi's just up after an hour's nap. I help Enid (Luned's sister) feed him his dinner – one of us gives him a spoonful of potatoes and peas and the other a spoonful of pudding, by turns! For now, I don't know of any other way to deal with the pretty little dear. Pretty? Sometimes he seems too handsome and loving and cheerful to be real – perish the thought! Just like his mother, everybody says. Hmmm!

JUNE THE 9TH: Behold: a week of brilliant, fiery, hot days – days like many I experienced when I was in France; and they're certainly a good bit warmer than we typically expect here. Turnabout is fair play, after all, considering February's exceptional cold, when the mountain ponies froze in their beds, and the birds' feet froze to the branches. A masterpiece of fine weather. Isn't this strange, though: a lot of folks are complaining about it. That's a shame! What about all those thousands and thousands of soldiers forced to fight in France, from three in the morning till eleven at night? Wouldn't you think the balmy weather comforts them a *little* bit at least?

JUNE THE 10TH: Tonight, some awful news – particularly awful in my opinion. Italy has just declared war. Yes, indeed; what a blow. For weeks, there've been signs, but nobody wanted to believe them. Now look! How in the world can Italy justify its war against France? Have they completely forgotten about the common pedigree between these two peoples? Or the great kindnesses of 1859-1860?[48] Or the shared traditions and civilizations of these two nations? What about Italy's centuries of struggle against Germany? Take Rome, for example – here's a city once sacked by barbarians, and now Italy is uniting herself with these very *same* barbarians in an alliance against her neighbor – against a people of her own blood and culture. O! Rome. You have sinned. You've gone mad! Even from the entirely materialistic and selfish standpoint of politics, you have lost your way. If Germany wins the war, what will be your fate in the Mediterranean Sea, in the Adriatic? When I think of you helping Germany not only to win the day – the *night*, rather – against France, but also to dismember her…well, it's just too blasphemous and dreadful to contemplate. I'm shivering with indignation.

JUNE 12TH: My disappointment and anger haven't diminished in the least – not yesterday, not today, neither morning nor evening. It's all becoming a nightmare, in fact. I'm waking up frequently at night, and my worries weigh heavily upon me. Today I arise only to read more about the aerial attack on Paris; about flesh-and-blood creation and masterpieces of stone and wood all being laid waste. Then there's the matter of half a million people attempting to flee the city. God of the Heavens – can't You do something? What's there left to say? To think? How well I recall my last hours in Paris, those first memorable hours of September 1939. I remember the very words that formed in my mind on that occasion: When will I see you again? And what will you look like?

Work has become a burden. Even the effort of putting my thoughts in order is oppressive. Just the same, I'm grateful for the work, for the students, for my children – grateful even for their clamor and their crying.

JUNE 13TH: The bad news continues. My darling Paris, city of cities, literary paradise, cradle of culture for the last several centuries, blessed daughter of humanity – you are in mortal danger. The barbarians are at your walls; the savage is at your gates. The Philistines thirst for your blood. Tomorrow – is it possible? – tomorrow the legions will descend upon your handsome streets, barge into your stately gardens, trample your elegance, crush your beauty. They will gnash their teeth against your plentiful churches, your masterpieces. What a horrendous thought. Let curses rain down upon them all!

June 14th: It is done. The Germans have reached Paris. O, sin! Where... where...where lies the blame? Who are the criminals responsible for all this? Is it that contemptible lot of politicians who call themselves the Third Republic – they with their bitter anti-clericalism, with their hostility to the army and their negligent shortsightedness? Of those few among you who are indeed great treasures – you ghostly shades of Thiers, Gambetta, Poincaré, Clemençeau[49] – where are you? Why didn't you sweep the "rotten rabble" into oblivion?

June 15th: I'm reading a description of Paris the way it was yesterday, as light and life were taking their leave and wretched darkness overwhelmed all. I'm preoccupied with this image all day long. If I happen to be reading about something else, the spectre of Paris rushes up before my eyes performing a *danse macabre* among the words on the page. When I walk to the College and pass through a field or a tended garden, there's that apparition of Paris once again. If I cock my head for even the briefest moment of contemplation, my breast heaves with all these overwhelming thoughts and feelings of grief for Paris' unmerciful fate.

There is one sole comfort: I remind myself that, for years now, I have loved Paris and France and all of the best things about them both – the brilliant, humane literature; the long tradition of high civilization; the centuries-old vitality of Catholic morality, thought and religion. And yet, at the very same time, I have hated her fickle, immoral, anticlerical politicians. How true, how prophetically true have been all the prescient writings of Maurras and Bainville and Daudet.[50] Bainville – with the shining, penetrating eyes and that cunning, cutting mind of his. Jacques Bainville – now lying in his grave, out of earshot of our woe. And as for Maurras? That poor, poor wretch. It is he who has so profoundly detested the Germans' barbarity – who has served his goddess France day in and day out with the passion and the purity of a saint. He is the one who warned his nation to beware the cataclysm that has by now engulfed her eastern borders! Where is he tonight? Why, he's been arrested for haranguing the politicians and for trying to enlighten his nation. He's already spent several stints in prison – and, yes, he's been condemned by the Church too, God bless him!

JUNE 16TH: Sunday – and a strange Sunday at that. It's eerily quiet; we don't hear so much as the peal of a bell from morning till night. And no newspaper to be found anywhere. After Sunday School, I take all the children, along with Enid, to pay Luned a visit. Today's their first time to go. They're very eager and a bit too talkative on the way down – carrying on about the new baby, about Mama. Then we arrive. Not five words out of any one of them for quite a while, in spite of their Mama's smiles. And Dewi hardly recognizes her, because he now confuses her with her sister Enid! In the end, though, he bounds into her arms. And the others pluck up the courage to ask, "Do we get to see the baby?"

"You certainly do; here he is! Well, do you like him?" They approach all together, but somewhat suspiciously. They gaze at him mutely for a moment, then smile at one another. "He's pretty, Mama."

"Can he speak?"

"No, not yet…and I don't yet know whether he'll be speaking Welsh or English," their mother says.

"O, he's crying, Mama."

On the way home, there's a lot of talk about the baby; and Mererid says, "I'd like to be a boy. If I write a letter to Jesus Christ, do you think he could turn me into a boy?"

When we reach the house, the woman next door asks the children,

"Did you see the baby? Was he pretty?"

"He was. We liked him." And in the same breath, Hywel says, "He cries in English." Then Mererid pipes up, "And Mama says if he speaks English, he won't get to come and live with us...or with you either, Mrs. Jones. He'll have to go live with Mrs. M., because it's English they speak in her house."

JUNE 17TH: The sun is glorious, so I hold one or two of my classes out in the open air. It's splendid.

After dinner, I attend the Monthly Meeting at Bwlan Chapel.[51] I've stopped rebelling against becoming a deacon, so now here I am gliding into office. Today, we are to be ordained, and a fellow deacon-elect and I are in a car belonging to yet a third member of our group. That's one glory associated with the office, at least – we get a chance to strike out into the countryside along winding lanes, between dense hedgerows, surrounded by lush meadows. We approach the small chapel. There's an awful lot of black in the roadway – elders, ministers, preachers. Black, the hue of choice today for both their sartorial and facial expressions. What's going on? Turns out they've just heard the one o'clock news: France has put down her arms. It's being whispered from door to door, from throng to throng, up and down the countryside. At times like this, you see how news travels, arrives at a destination and mingles about – how it sobers, saddens, disheartens and floors everyone who hears it. This sunny day has turned thickly overcast, sullen, calamitous. It's just a single cloud; but in spite of its distance from us across the English Channel, it's still too close at hand. People

Glimpses of Life in Wales

are as lost as if the Last Judgment had descended. As if a nimbus had been dispatched from the Dominion of Doom – it won't retreat; won't lift away; won't scatter off. This then is how the lights of France were extinguished in Arfon [North Wales] – and in full view, no less, of Dinas Din*lleu*.[52]

We head into the Chapel. A trembling old man is praying intensely, frightfully hard; and his quavering voice reverberates over the heads of the congregation. The atmosphere is full of tension and oppression and tribulation. One spark, and the place would erupt in bonfire. But there is no spark. Instead, we new deacons are asked to "relate" or "tell about" our experiences. God only knows how strange, how superficial this all is. Such foolish talk! May He forgive us! Next, we're questioned about the Institutions of the Methodist Union. Vanity of vanities. Finally, another old man – and what a day it is for old men, from Bwlen to Bordeaux! – rises to exhort us. He's wise, he's tedious; he's tedious, he's wise....

Back in Bangor, I see two people chatting over here, three more over yonder. They're in the street, in the shops – everyone's tongues are burning with indistinct snatches of commentary: "…after word of the fighting…"; "…thousands of lives lost…"; "…all in vain…"; "…want to shoot the whole lot – Chamberlain, Baldwin, MacDonald[53] – every last one of them!"

As I make my way to town, I read a letter that came this morning. I didn't have time to get to it earlier. I open it; it's from one of my former students – another "A" effort, 12 pages long this time! I read on: he's apologizing, not for its length but for delaying so long to write. He thanks me for trying to comfort him. And he's at greater peace with circumstances now than previously. He's met with several soldiers who've returned from Dunkirk, and he's riveted by the way they bring to life the immediacy of the battlefield. But what he can't understand is their impatience *"to return better equipped to give the dirty Hun what he deserves.*[54]

> *"…The futility of it, when men think peace will come by killing Germans…Many thousands of recruits have passed through here since I arrived. I have had news of one or two that I trained, being already killed. Not at all a comforting thought. Not that I pretend to be deeply touched. Only, it makes me feel that I have had a hand in their killing. But who hasn't these days? A world of killers. I have shuddered to hear the gurgling in a sheep's throat, as it bled in the slaughter house. I killed one when I was in school…How would you feel if it were your daily work to teach boys the best way to kill with a bayonet? That has been added to my list of duties now. I have to teach them how the bayonet and the flesh cling to each other, making extraction difficult. I have to work them into a fury of madness; get them to scream and shout!, teach them to curse and swear with the uttermost vileness. It looks silly (I like the word 'daft') and indeed I am often thinking that it is just silly. Not horrible and priggish, just silly."*

Other thoughts occur to him: *"Is death in mass more awful really than poverty and ignorance, and the mass slime and dirtiness of our day to day life?"*

An attempt to comfort himself follows, and he's determined to "be a good soldier." He is thankful for what he has – life, health and this: *"For the first time in my life I am able to help my mother and father to live."* He's grateful for this friends, and he includes me amongst them: *"You were generous to me at Coll. You are kind to listen to my babble now…It would be good to be taught by you again…Life is still worth living."* And he ends by asking me for another letter.

I shiver a bit to read a letter like this – today of all days. It certainly isn't necessary for him to be so thankful. After all, wasn't I once something other than a "consoler of affliction" to these boys when exam day came around?

JUNE 19TH: More grievous news yesterday. And today, this: I see that Rennes has fallen. So the Germans have reached calm, quiet, peaceful Brittany. It almost feels as if they were in Wales. I recall that time the bull rushed my youngest sister as she led the cattle home for milking. She hid in the darkness of the hedgerow, and she felt its breath upon her; and all the while, there was nothing I could do. That's how I feel today – utterly useless.

I receive a remarkably tender letter from my Breton friend Loeiz Herrieu in which he thanks me for *A Fortnight's Diary*. He wrote on the 9th of the month – 10 days ago, when the massacre was still some distance from his country. How wildly this explosion has ripped through Europe. Today, the Germans are in the vicinity of his own house, that small island of bountiful hospitality. What will happen? Please, God, don't let anything happen to him!

JUNE THE 20TH: A friend wants me to accompany him to Llandudno. At first, I don't want to; then I have second thoughts. Can Dewi and Enid come? I ask. "By all means." Very well, then; they'll join us! It's a pleasant day, and the countryside is all spruced up for summer. But the view from the road is obstructed by the embankments and barricades people are putting up everywhere. And then, barbed wire[55] on top of that. There's no escape – nowhere to hide from my misgivings and concerns, from my fears and doubts. Even though Dewi is sitting on my knees talking a blue streak, I can't seem to get these thoughts out of my mind. We arrive and stop for tea. I've no taste for it. English good-for-nothings are everywhere; so is their wanton dancing and drunken music. The seashore is thick with people, and they're living it up. As far as I'm concerned, it's just a flood-tide of sinfulness. And to think there's all this lighthearted nonsense and carefree self-indulgence going on, while at this very moment millions of people are suffering the most abysmal fate. Am I losing my sense of perspective?

J∪ne the 21st: [56] On my way home from the College, at about one o'clock, I hear the noisy chatter of radio broadcasts coming from every house I pass by. It's the same thing every day now. At one… again at six…the streets go empty; and men and women "put on the news" with a trembling hand. Today, I hear the occasional shout here and there about the peace terms Germany is dictating to France. It's as if the noise were splashing loudly through open windows right into the middle of the road. I don't know a thing about what's going on, really. And I don't ask anyone, either. Besides, there isn't anyone around to ask, except for a few people scurrying off towards the shelter of their own homes. Off to their damn houses with them, then. Let me have the street all to myself so I can stride as sprightly as I please. Tomorrow will be soon enough for me to get all the news. I *already* know too much.

It's mid-afternoon. I'm going out to fetch Luned home today, after spending a fortnight and a half without her. Who's happier she's home – she or we? Dewi is truly full of himself, and he's droning, "Ma-ma, Ma-ma," over and over again. In all fairness, he does welcome the baby too; but he also snatches his small pram away. The other children greet mother and baby a little more quietly, but no less enthusiastically. So here were are, all together again – a family of seven now. And we've got lots of grief, trouble, pain and fatigue to look forward to – and, without a doubt, noise. But there'll be lots of pleasure, as well; and many full and amusing days. I'll be grateful for them all, every single one of them.

June the 23rd: Sunday – off to Chapel, where J.P. Davies of Porthmadog is preaching. He prays intensely, most intensely – "Almighty and Compassionate God…" He beseeches; he implores; he pours out his soul. He prays *for Wales*. Then the floodgates open, and tears stream from my eyes – tears of joy, of sympathy, of compassion. No one else is praying for Wales! They're all praying "for our country" instead; and God knows that Wales isn't meant to be included in *that* expression. "Our country…our leaders"; that's *their* tripe – over in England and in Parliament. There's no denomination or church I know of praying for Wales – not for the misery she's suffering, not for her leaders nor for her writers! God bless any man who dares do *that*!

There's news from all over: Dijon, Lyon, Limoges, Rennes, Nantes, St. Malo, Lorient – cities and towns I love; and as they capitulate, they fall under enemy control. Towns I know even better, like Quimper and Morlaix – they're feeling the scorch of the flame, the brunt of the wrath. The very homes of bosom-friends – Vallêe, Even, Goaziou, Gourvil, Herrieu – have already been seized perhaps. Today, it's Lorient…tomorrow, it will be Hennebont, just three miles from Herrieu's home! It might as well be the Coming of the Apocalypse! How has it possibly come to pass that France – the most genial, enlightened, brilliant and cultured of nations – should deserve such affliction and subjugation?

June the 24th: I read the terms of armistice. They're harsh and oppressive. Unacceptable, I say to myself, wholly unacceptable. And yet, look: Pétain has agreed to them. Is it due to lack of resolve? Has he fallen out of love with France? Hardly. He just happens to know more than we do about the entire *débacle*. What's being said and published in England is simply loathsome: There's a subtle implication that France ought to continue fighting, if only for England's sake. Pure selfishness – in full bloom. What would England do in similar straits? What if Germany had attacked England before France, had defeated and floored her first? Would England then show the slightest concern for France or for some supposedly hallowed agreement?[57]

JUNE THE 25TH: I'm lecturing for the last time this college year – the long-awaited "last class." There have been several boys in each of my classes who've already left for the army. The ones still here are but a *gweddill* [remnant], even if they're still fairly numerous. "…And there is always a serious and startled look upon the faces of the remnant, as though…"[58] They behave like a remnant too – a remnant waiting their turn; unhappy, uncertain, unsteady. "Cynddylan's hall is dark tonight…"[59]

JUNE THE 2_TH: [60] Now we see Italy's terms of armistice. They too are harsh, even though the Italians have scarcely fought at all. They're merely profiting from France's utter helplessness. Shades of old Mazzini[61] again! And yet, Pétain accepts the terms. Did he even complain? This is also very hard to understand. People all around me are fuming and raging. *Patati, Patata!*[62] But what do we really know for sure? Nothing, except this: There's a lot of anger in France directed towards England, which didn't provide the assistance she had promised – soldiers, air support and so forth. In addition to anger, there's also depression, disgust, disappointment and wounded pride – to say nothing of the suffering, the wailing, the confusion and the desperate attempts to escape under cover of fog and smoke and darkness of night. Then, there are people like General de Gaulle urging, indeed, demanding that the battle continue at all costs.[63] Is he another Gambetta?…another *"fou furieux"* [crazy fool], to borrow Thiers' phrase? If not, what is he?

What about Charles Maurras? Is he free? In custody? He, Daudet, the whole brilliant lot of them – what's their status? All their dreams are in shambles! How can they – of all people – put up with terms so punitive, so insulting to France's dignity? It's simply incredible, really, that exemplary soldiers like Pétain and Weygand could agree to terms like these – then compel their fellow Frenchmen to abide by them too!

JUNE THE 29TH: A letter. On the outside of the envelope are these words, in English: "*No service, return to sender. Opened by Examiner 443.*" My letter has come back – the one I wrote on the 12th of the month to my friend Gourvil in Brittany. The curtain has descended. I hear nothing more from Brittany. My world is contracting; my horizons are narrowing. There are no papers from France, no letters from Brittany. What torment to the spirit. How long till there's more news from Brittany? I'm afraid a long silence is in store for me. What about the fates of my friends Gourvil, Herrieu, Valêe…? And what about the others – Mordrel, Debauvais, Lainê…? Will they now realize their goal of an independent Brittany? Will Mordrel, or one of them anyway, become her leader, her dictator – under Hitler?

The Fifth Chapter

July 1st: Troubling news: Russia and Japan, are raising their tails, so to speak – like horses getting ready to jump. Everyone is consumed with greed – like wild, rapacious beasts. There's no sense of responsibility, or fairness, or honor; and France's disappearance is already bearing bitter fruit.

July the 4th: Here's this morning's eight o'clock news: The English fleet has just attacked the French fleet in North Africa.[64] How disgusting! England has gone from accusing France to fending for herself. And keep in mind – only a few weeks back, all the English papers were prating on about this supposedly indissoluble union of hearts between our two countries! France lies in a pool of her own blood in the dust. And now, people are positively climbing over each other's backs for an opportunity to curse her, insult her, trample her underfoot. That's the Englishman's way of course: to thank whomever fights by his side, until that ally falters, then falls. In her wounded condition, France suggested that both countries negotiate a joint-armistice and share in the suffering, in the occupation. Then, in the depths of her woe, France sought to keep her fleet out of German hands. And she succeeded too – on paper, at any rate. Be that as it may, it was the gesture of a noble nation. Yet no one seems to understand that!

July the 6th: The College has closed, and all my papers are graded. The holidays! At two o'clock, the Denbighshire Conference kicks off at Colwyn Bay under the auspices of the Movement for Safeguarding Welsh Culture. I'm scheduled to speak; and I'm glad to do so, because I haven't spoken in public since before the start of the war.

I may have a bad cold, and I'm running a fever; but so what? I'm going anyway. The Bishop of St. Asaph, Mr. Morgan Humphreys and Sir Artemus Jones[65] are also speaking. We're in the great hall of the Middle School, and the place is full. Sir Artemus presides. It's the first time I've ever met him. We chat briefly beforehand – about Owain Glyn Dŵr, the Tudor Period and so forth. His conversation is more congenial than his demeanor; and his Welsh is a little spotty – too much foreign accent. What's with that accent anyway? The Bishop is a no-show, nor does he bother to send an explanation! M.H. speaks first; he's relaxed, sensible, rational, rather ineloquent but not without wit. His resolution is seconded by Mr. D.R. Hughes, of Old Colwyn. I'm next. I'm well received (or so I suppose). Nothing much new in what I have to say, unless perhaps it's the emphasis I place upon the righteous, virtually sacrosanct nature of the oath we've all taken to work towards safeguarding, even rescuing, Welsh culture. "We – you and I – who take this oath in the name of every generation that has preceded us, are honor-bound to deliver our culture intact into the future." Applause. I don't hide anything; I'm feeling happy, truly joyful. I half-believe I'm *living* for the moment – that I'm bringing this moment to *life*. Am I deluding myself? Maybe. There's no question I'm tugging at heartstrings. It's delightful to have a chance to encounter some of my old students and some of the Party members[66] I haven't seen since, well, Noah's flood! I take tea with D.R.H.[67] for a few exquisite hours. I get home in good cheer – I'm in too good a mood, in fact, to nod off to sleep for quite some time. What a simpleton I am!

JULY THE 10TH: News of the worst, most troubling disasters has stopped. But so has our sense of fellow-feeling. Fear, anxiety and suspicion have taken its place. A wave of distrust has come over us – every piece of news, every whispered rumor, even one's neighbor is now suspect. Ideal circumstances for the Men of the Fifth Column.[68] People see them, imagine them everywhere. Ferreting out spies is the daily preoccupation of everyone around me. Not far from here, two soldiers are keeping watch on a family that's as innocent as the angels of Seventh Heaven. Nightmare suspicion is in the air – even in children's conversations. When Lowri runs crying into the house from the midst of playing outside, I ask, "What's wrong?"

"A boy is screaming at me."

"What's he saying?"

"*Your father is a German Spy.*"[69]

Not in vain does the radio cast seeds of madness into the airwaves every night. Bangor has certainly been infected, but only somewhat! The Education Committee for Anglesey has decided to "release" – to *release*, mind you – a conscientious objector from his teaching responsibilities. He's the only C.O. in the district, and he's a likeable boy and a good teacher. I know him; he's a former student. And he has no father, to boot! What wretches you are! Where's the sense, fools; where's the common sense?

JULY THE 12TH: I get a chance to turn my back on town life for a while, and on townspeople too. I'm spending three days in the calm, quiet countryside between the small villages of Talywern and Aberhosan. I arrive at Cilwinllan, the home of an aunt and uncle of mine[70] – and what a charming home it is indeed. It feels like I'm sailing on a sea of kindness. This is a perfectly peaceful place, awash with the burble and chatter of flowing streams. I walk through cloudbursts; I ramble; I run. I soak up the sounds of the rushing waters and the bleating sheep; I'm almost completely at one with the peacefulness that sighs inaudibly beneath, through, within the clamor of the landscape. All about me are verdant seas of fern, wooded glens, small random hamlets, shepherds climbing and farm girls calling after their dogs and sheep. Just as it has always been! O, how agreeable it all is! Everything is charming – a district of sheer delight. I rise in the morning and laze about as luxuriantly as I please. I watch idly as my uncle shears some wandering lambs. Rays of sunlight descend through the treetops into the stillness of the farmyard. I go to Chapel on Sunday morning and savor the sounds of the sheep bleating in faint counterpoint to our lofty devotions to the saints. *Monday morning*: I strike out for *Cae-tu-cefn-i'r-Beudy* ["Field-behind-the-Cowshed"], where I sit on the seat of a hay-mowing machine. I look out, amazed, over the small, sloping fields all bright and green. I see groves of trees in a narrow valley. On the summit of one of the farthest ridges, I can make out the tiny village of Darowen smiling down at me affectionately amidst a raiment of white and green. The soft shapeliness of the mountain known as Aran Fawddwy muses in silence beneath a billowing shroud of mist. Off to my side, the man from Rhiwgoch farm and his son are mowing hay upon a narrow strip of steep, craggy land. There's less and less and less…until the last thin swathe disappears entirely. The son takes the tractor to another field, while the father stays behind to tidy up with his scythe. It's a gentle, quiet morning. As the scent of new-mown hay diffuses, the voice of a three-year-old child chimes in from nearby. She approaches her dad with some difficulty through the felled swathes. He lays his scythe down and bends to his knee, then draws the little girl to him. He strokes her; pecks her with kisses. I see her pretty green frock merging into his cotton waistcoat, and her yellow-blond hair spreads out over his tan-dark arms. It's such a charming scene! Here, my fellow countrymen, is your genuine birthright in all its glory. Here is your throne and your consolation with which to endure the interminable perfidy arrayed against you. My Wales, my own people…I love you

Glimpses of Life in Wales

beyond the power of words to say. During every dark hour, still you bend to your daily toil, sustained by oceans of virtue and seas of compassion. Hail to thee, dearest Wales.

Tomorrow, I must turn back unwillingly and leave behind the people, the experiences and the vistas that have served as balm for my heart. I'll be back to see you again before the end of the holidays. Once more, you have restored in me a lost vitality.

JULY THE 17TH: I sit down to work. There's a lot to do, in spite of the holidays. I'm combing through the official records of Star Chamber proceedings, scores of them. Reading them, I hear the moans of the common folk during the Tudor period. I'm examining wills by the dozen and reading through letters pertaining to my own family which date from 1795 onward. I'm trying to put all these things into some semblance of order. I'm also reading the Old Tailor,[71] the Old Stanzas,[72] *Y Wisg Sidan*,[73] the poetry of Villemarque and Jean Calloc'h, and so forth. There's produce to gather from the garden, which needs a bit of tidying up and hedging here and there. Occasionally, I'm off to the countryside – to Pen Mynnydd, Y Gesail Gyfarch, Pentre Ariannel, Plas Iolyn and the like. And with all that, before I know it, the summer holidays will have flown right by!

JULY THE 22ND: A trip to the countryside today. A friend wants to take me to Ysbyty Ifan. It'll be a good opportunity to get in a bit of hill-walking and to visit the home of *y Doctor Coch* [the Red Doctor] and his son Thomas Prys.[74] We head out from Nant Ffrancon at about 9:30. My friend, A.R.,[75] is a talented and witty fellow. He's telling me about Maes Geirchen, Maes Gwenith and Maes Brynar[76] in the district of Penrhyn, which he considers proof-positive of a three-field crop rotation system in Wales. Then he brings up the rape of Penrhyn and Y Faenol during the last century: First, the crofters enclosed the common lands, leaving only a narrow buffer of mountain ridge, which they called a "stocking," between them and the landed estates. Then, the owners of the estates colluded to imply, fraudulently, that the government was looking for a way to expropriate these remaining high commons. They persuaded the crofters to contribute one shilling each to a defense fund – the so-called Shilling for Defense. With that, their lordships were able to claim ownership of the commons for themselves, in that the collected shillings represented lease payments by the crofters. Pretty crafty, eh?

We discuss the war a bit. And we climb, up past the road that turns off to Dolwyddelan. At the intersection, we come upon a boy driving a sow before him. With a smile my friend says, "There you see the one thing that'll never change, even if all the empires go up in cinders."

A little to the far side of Pentre Foelas I descend towards a gate and path leading to Plas Iolyn. We compare the time and agree to meet back at Ysbyty Ifan at about four o'clock. I put my feet to the ground in earnest now and strike out over the fields. Sheep and cattle are all around me, and everything is quiet. There's a field of oats here, a field of clover hay there and great stone enclosures everywhere. I breathe in the atmosphere and reach the manor house. Plas Iolyn is a handsome place, and several bits of it perhaps date back to the days of the old Doctor himself: the great timber trusses, for example, and the shiny oaken stairs. Something tells me that the tower was where he kept his prisoners. There's a massive granary, with the date 1572 scratched into one of its crossbeams. I press on – to Giler, past a half-mown hay field. There's a man standing where the trail passes through a gap; his hay knife hangs at his back. He's got a very suspicious look on his face. I say hello: "*Dydd da*" [Good day].

"'Tis good for me to hear you speaking Welsh, Sir."

"And why wouldn't I?"

"Expecting a German, I was…and thinking to put this here knife into him."

He breaks out laughing, and he walks with me towards the estate's farmhouse. Along the way, he shows me the *"Get-Ws"* [Gate House], as he calls it, as well as the various gates and walls around the park, the bolts of firewood, the parlor and its rich paneling, etc. They are sure signs of wealth and high-living; you can almost feel the shadow of the Doctor's presence. At the worn, stone threshold of the cowshed, the fellow stops and points: "There's you some traces of the footsteps of the Red Doctor's own horse!"

I take my leave and trudge across a soggy peat bog towards the "old road," down which lies the end of my trail at Ysbyty Ifan. Opposite the churchyard there's a pub – the *Tŷ'n y Porth* [Gate House].[77] I enter – no! not the pub; the churchyard. Wales is thick with churchyards, of course; and in this one, there are three ancient yews and a handsome church with a fetching bell tower. The church door is locked, but I manage to open it anyway! Very interesting: What first catches your eyes are the sculptures, and they're all lying down: There's Lowri, wife of Rhys Fawr; there's Rhys Fawr himself; and there's Robert ap Rhys. The mother is intact; the father is missing his legs; and the son is headless. Here they are, all together – from the high life to the lowly grave. There's no reference to the Red Doctor anywhere, nor to his son.

I go back outside into the road. Two men are working lethargically on a house, and one seems to fancy himself some kind of poet. There's a funny look about him. "An old smithy was this 'ere house," he pipes up. "Cattle were shoed 'ere on their way to England. That old roadhouse down by the bridge there was a sanctuary in the old time. 'Ere's an old saying about the place:

> *"Caled fe ar lawer gŵr,*
> *Nes cyrraedd pont y Cletwr."*
> [Hard times they were for lots of men,
> Until the wood-beam bridge arrived.]

"A sanctuary for *robbers*, friend!" I say.

" Yup, perhaps," he says; "and bards."

"Bards? What bards?"

"Why, 'ere's you one," says his mate. These are the first words he's uttered so far.

Taking his cue, the bard concurs. "Perfectly true, it is. I've published five books…poetry each one…sixpence apiece. 'Tis 500 copies I've sold."

And the titles of these books?

Harp of the Working-man, Flowers on the Grave; and so forth. To think – I've never heard the first word about any of them!

At the bridge, I sit against the handrail. My thoughts wander idly over things surrounding me – green fields slanting down to the river; white clouds marching by as if in procession; two butterflies hovering over a bed of peas and beans. A girl is fetching water from the spring; and Lord Penrhyn's gamekeeper is descending from the high hills. Everything is profoundly still. The river is chattering; those lazy fellows back there are whistling. There's mirth and commotion as children empty out of the schoolhouse. "How many of you are there?" I ask. *"Twenti Ffôr,"* one of them says.

"What's that? You must have meant *'pedwar ar hugain,'* surely?"[78]

"Yes, sir."

The gamekeeper is now close enough to overhear: "About 15 years ago, when I was in school, there were *sicsti sefn*[79] of us."

"There you go again! – you and your *sicsti sefn*." Declining standards everywhere you turn – not only in the number of children attending school but also in the very language they're supposed to be counted in. Ysbyty Ifan – a sanctuary? A sanctuary for what!

My friend has arrived. We head over to Dylasau for some refreshments and a spectacular meal. The way home takes us through Llanrwst and Trefriw after a truly rejuvenating day out in the countryside.

August the 4th: My birthday.[80] How terrifying. How embarrassing. I've still not accomplished anything of importance in my life – now *that's* a sobering thought. I have to smile when I recall that, as children, our birthday present was a boiled egg – and we thought the world of it. We take advantage of my birthday, in fact, to baptize the baby – at the Cathedral. (Luned is Church; I'm Chapel). We sail on down with the whole brood in tow; and the children are a little anxious. We name the baby – Owain ab Emrys Bebb.[81] He doesn't cry; not so much as a peep out of his mouth. He endures the reading, and the water startles him awake; he's wide-eyed, but he still doesn't fuss. Dewi wanders about, pacing like a little lion. He's shouting, "Da-da…Ma-ma…Bab-an" into the hollow emptiness of the church – and in front of Owain Gwynedd's tomb.[82]

August the 7th: Dewi's birthday – he's two years old today and as handsome, cheerful and fleet-footed as ever. There he is in his little blue suit, with curly blond hair framing an innocent face that's the very image of flesh-and-blood perfection. A scratch-baked cake for him at teatime displays the words "Happy Birthday" between two lighted candles. He blows out both with a single breath! A stout fellow, to be sure. He can be very amusing at times. The day before yesterday, for example, he chewed a handful of cascara [laxative] pills that he scrounged up somewhere. He can be a remarkable pest too. Once, he spilled half a bottle of ink all over the front of my manuscript for a new book about Brittany. I would have cut off the heads of everyone in the house if I thought I could've gotten away with it!

August the 30th: I've kept my promise: Here I am back at Cilwinllan, for the third time this summer. On my second trip, I walked over the hills to Llanbrynmair. This time, I'm going over to Tregaron for a week. It was awfully difficult to leave my young family this time round, particularly considering the state of the world just now. It has really pulled at my heartstrings, leaving them behind like that – Dewi most of all, perhaps! I can just see the reproachful pout distorting that face of his, pretty as a pearl. As I set out, I'm rebuking myself and feel like a scoundrel, but the farther along I get on my journey, the more my pangs ease. When I see Aberglaslyn Bridge and Tal-y-llyn Lake, my heart jumps for joy. I send a hasty word back to Luned from Machynlleth cautioning her to keep an eye on Dewi – as if there were any danger that she'd ignore *any* of the children. I come down into Talywern, and keep walking along the *wtra* [sheep track][83] to Cilwinllan. I ramble and stride through the fields. When I hear a tractor harvesting grain, I head for the sound and help bind a sheaf or two before shocking [i.e., setting] them on end. Friday, Saturday, Sunday – the days disappear like a pleasant dream. They simply vanish, waiting to be recalled at some later date when something or other triggers my memory. I'll be leaving Lowri here so she can run around between Cilwinllan and Llwyngronfa playing with her cousins. Isn't she the lucky one!

September the 2nd: How well I remember this day last year.[84] Today, I'm leaving Cilwinllan for Tregaron. I'll get to help with the grain harvest if I'm not too late. And I'm not – the corn's all been cut, but only a little's been gathered up so far. It's perfect weather for this sort of work.

September the 4th: In the morning, everyone heads out to lay the *stacanau* [the shocks][85] down so they can dry in the sun before they're gathered up in the afternoon. Air ships – six, ten maybe – whiz by very low overhead, panicking the cattle into a gallop. After midday dinner, my brother, three farmhands and I return to the fields with three gambrels.[86] Out in the field, I'm lifting corn sheaves onto the cart. I pull off my shirt and more besides. There's nothing left but a scrap of cotton about my loins. Up with the sheaves – one, two, three, all of us together, and we complete a full load. "That's enough, Arthur!"

The next one! The carts and the loads follow one after the other like an unimpeded stream until it's time for tea. I'm thankful for the break, and for the apple tart. Then we're at it again tossing sheaves once more. We're all short of breath, since there's always a new gambrel in the field even before we've finished loading the last one. There's no time to utter a word, or even draw a breath almost. I'm tired after every load now – bone tired, in my right arm, my flanks and, especially, the palms of my hands. But we keep up the same pace until seven o'clock. What a relief! We count the loads – 14 or 15. Not bad, considering how far the field is from the house and how scattered the sheaves are. Back to the house, and I do my best to disguise my fatigue. Actually, I feel like I'm almost ready to get back to work. But not tonight, thank you very much.

SEPTEMBER 6TH: A fine, misty rain – clammy and unpleasant weather all morning yesterday. We weren't able to gather in any of the harvest. A very, very quiet day, which suited me just fine!

But today is a perfect day to be working. I'm completely refreshed. And, besides, the sheaves are all standing today. "Pitching" them will be child's play. Let's get to it! Once again, it's off with the clothes, up with the sheaves. Time passes by in a flash! – the same again all through the afternoon; and I'm not tired at all. I've come into my own. Now, we're finishing every load *before* the next empty cart reaches the field. That's some feat, let me tell you! Seven o'clock arrives before we even know it. Sixteen loads. And if one horse hadn't run away in the middle of a load, there'd be even more. Only eight loads left. We'll get those in tomorrow with no trouble at all.

SEPTEMBER THE 14TH: I've been back in Bangor for several days now and hard at work again. Today is a great day – it's Hywel's and Mererid's birthday, from dawn to dusk. They're making a racket before any of us has even contemplated opening our eyes. So we're obliged to wake up and listen to all the commotion and enthusiasm running wild. It gets louder yet once they've received some presents in the post and had their breakfast. Then, they're outside, carrying on like two cockerels and crowing about their fifth birthday to everyone in the street. They gambol and prance about all the day long, and Dewi and Lowri envy their wildness. By teatime, Luned has baked them a birthday cake and crowned it with five candles and plenty of sugar-icing – in spite of war-time rules and rations!

SEPTEMBER 20TH: A new college year begins. Boys and girls of the first year have come back for their second – girls in their full complement, boys numbering fewer than 15. They'll spend the first three weeks student-teaching in the schools. We faculty members will follow along to watch and listen to them.

Today, I head out and have a word with the headmistress of one of the schools. I'm surprised to see so many sluggish and weary children.

"I'm surprised as well, but they say it's like that everywhere."

"And how many would you say are behaving like that?"

"About a third of the children."

"Hmmm… That's quite a high proportion, isn't it? Why so, do you think?"

"Mostly, they come from poor homes – where they don't get enough attention, food and so forth. Among the smallest ones, even their bodies are suffering – to say nothing about their brains."

"Do you think it's as bad as all that?"

"I certainly do! Worse yet, almost all of them are Welsh! And because the Welsh happen to be the poorest folk around here, the English officials treat them just like menials – as if they held them beneath contempt. Here's another thing for you: These weary children are then sent along to Middle School, whereas the others go to Shire School.[87] They're kept apart – and these young Welsh children are shaping up to be – just like their fathers – mere water-bearers for the others; the Welsh serving the English…even in this day and age. That's how these rôles are perpetuated – a gulf that refuses to narrow."

What a fiendish cycle our Education System persists in handing down. How wretched our children are! How wretched their education is!

I have a similar chat with the headmaster of the Middle School, a dear, gracious, most cultivated man. We discuss the Shire School.

"O! There's no connection between them and us! At such and such a teachers' meeting the while back, none of them came!

They're completely detached from us…above us." So much for the Welsh Education System! Just another infernal machine! The Welsh *Un*education System is more like it.

S℮ptember 25th: It's about half-past eight in the evening. Luned and I are in the kitchen eating supper, and the children are sleeping. The sound of a heavy thud echoes from afar, and the door rattles. I'm stunned.

"A bomb has fallen somewhere!" Luned says. We go outside. True enough…between us and Llechwedd Isaf; and over Bangor Mountain and back towards the Carneddi Range, the entire cloudy sky is dancing with lights, brilliant flashes and fire. The fireworks travel across the sky in increasing numbers, then flash like lightning. A boom of thunder follows a moment later. Above the long streak of random flashes, three, now four great disks of light stand still. Then they start expanding and moving towards us, swaying as they approach. They're like the awful, seething eyes of a giant. They pause again, pull away, retreat slowly and disappear.

For minutes – it felt like quite a long time, but it wasn't really – the air was crowded with these strange, frenzied apparitions; and our hearts filled with worry and fear. We were gazing, it seemed, into the face of dreadful Death itself. In the darkness, we knew that Death had in fact descended upon some districts very near us and that people – our brothers and sisters, all of them Welsh of course – were being consumed in a furnace of fire.

"I'd get into the house if I were you," says a man next door.

We wait a minute longer, then go inside. Quietly, and for the first time tonight, Luned and I ask one another in all seriousness: Will we be next – together with our five children? Pwllheli has already been hit. Rhos has also been badly hit. It was somewhere else near us tonight. Will Bangor be next?

SEPTEMBER 26TH: I'm grateful for dawn, for the morning – for the light of day that follows night – for the light that banishes darkness and fear and trembling. I step outside into the streets of the town. People in twos and threes are talking to one another. Everybody's visibly thankful and completely unscathed by the bombing. Everybody's commiserating over Death's visitation amongst our neighbors in Bethesda and Llanllechid. Four killed, someone says; six wounded. "They're over at Bangor Hospital right over yonder." Our neighbors in Bethesda, of all people![88] Who could be more completely undeserving? What could possibly have been accomplished? Who would ever have imagined it?

The Sixth Chapter

October the 2nd: Another letter from a former student – B., this time, who's English. He thanks me for my own letter:

"It gave me immense pleasure to be reminded of Bangor, which to-day seems so very, very, far away. But it made me sad too. It reminded me of the days we had spent in building a lot of very beautiful ideas, while we had lived there tucked away amidst the trees of the Straits, sheltered from the hard face of the world…"

He feels it's a shame that students don't have much experience of the real world before coming to College; otherwise, there'd be a better foundation for all their learning (an excellent notion indeed!)…

"They would have a firmer basis on which to build their ideas. For my part, I feel that I have had to start all over again since I have left College. It is so easy when one is living College life, with but slight financial worries, to take security from mundane worries, and beauty for granted…to start building on the assumption that manna will fall from heaven at one's feet, and that beauty blossoms by some law of the universe. What I have learnt since, from my experience and not from books, is that what man cares about first is bread – with butter, if possible… This came as a sort of disillusionment to me. Now it appears perfectly natural. Perhaps I expected that men should live like angels, or that some divine providence would look after our bodies and all we had to bother about were our souls. Now it appears to me that the mind is dependent upon the well-being of the body. From this there arise two ideas. First that culture must be the monopoly of those people who either have an independent income or who are able to have a fair amount of leisure time…Secondly it seems to be a fundamental stumbling block to the practise of Christianity. It seems that we can never escape from the tyranny of the body. Its demands are there and must be met before you can start thinking about selling

your goods and giving the proceeds to the nearest charitable institution. And if you live in a world where you can't feed your body without swindling your neighbour, you will swindle your neighbour and exist, or you don't do the swindle and you die, and your responsibilities — mother, wife or children — die with you, all hoping to go to heaven.

"The utterances of the Church during the war seem to justify this attitude. Remembering your injunction that the Church is a human institution...it still seems obvious that the business of the Church these days is to justify any action the State may wish to do. The strictest of sabbatarians in peace time suddenly discover that the demands of necessity may be acceded to in war time and that it may be quite justifiable to bomb Berlin off the face of the earth...

"Since I was called up I have given over the problem that faced us twelve months ago and it is still unsolved. It appears to me that I have done nothing but drift into the army. I have made no decisions. I see nothing clearly, but live in a mist of confused and inchoate ideas...I was completely torn at the time of registering for service — between what I believe and my responsibilities to my parents. I could see clearly enough that a refusal to accept service would not solve the issue of war and peace; but the glory of it was that I could say, after following a properly logical argument — the war is not my responsibility it's yours, who care to fight it; go ahead and blow yourselves to bits!...Then it dawned upon me that this was pure escapism...I felt that I could not stand aside from the conflict...and had no right to. I literally did not know what to do...I had doubts, all kinds of doubts...and in this very confused state of mind I just took the line of least resistance — and here I am.

"What is there to do but turn to one of the thousand and one drugs that are for sale on the market, to forget, forget, for a while, the problems that remain unsolved, unsolvable...Have we any control over our actions in the long run?... Have principles, ideals, ultimately any reality?...I have become sick of asking questions, sick of self-searching. The one being from whom I wish to escape is myself — and there seems to be none..."

I'm quoting extensively, but that's by no means all there is. Do you see the quandary these boys are in? Can't you just feel their plain-spoken sincerity, born of rank oppression of the spirit? They've been cast out of gossamer halls and into the bowels of fiends! I feel responsible for each one of them.

OCTOBER THE 5TH: My undergraduates have finished their three weeks of student-teaching; and some new students have just arrived. I saw the boys about three days ago. They're very young, younger than usual in fact – some don't even look 18 yet. Is it possible they might not get to stay the whole term? There's certainly a look of innocence about them. They're shy and awkward – for the time being. When they get better acquainted with one another, and with us on faculty, they'll soon be brave enough and full of their oats! It's amusing to watch them loosen up around one another and grow more confident – and more daring. Good for them.

I'm lecturing to the girls today, and some want to take Welsh. There are about 35 of them, and they're from every shire in Wales save three – Radnorshire, Breconshire and Monmouth. How interesting! Being amongst them, I feel like I'm able to keep tabs on almost all of Wales on a regular basis, from one day's class to the next. That's why these hours spent lecturing are so special to me. In the company of these girls – the boys too – I feel like I'm present in dozens of Welsh homes. It's a splendid privilege, if I do say so myself. All of Wales, before my very eyes.

OCTOBER 11TH: It's about half-past five in the evening. I'm still at the College. I'm here for the night, in fact, and have been for a week. It's my turn to be "on duty"! Every five weeks or so, we faculty members alternate being in charge. I arrive around five-o'clock teatime and stay over to "keep the peace," so to speak. Supper's served about 8:30; roll-call is 9:45. Then we read a selection from Scripture, sing a hymn and say a short prayer. It's "lights-out" at 10:30. In the morning, we begin again!

Tonight, we no sooner finish our tea when the boys vanish like mice into their rooms. An airplane zooms past, very low. Then there's the shrill howl of the Porthaethwy siren from across the Menai Strait. I leap to the window, peering intently and straining to hear. The College siren wails, which manages to shatter peace and quiet throughout this whole, vast dormitory. Doors rattle open, and the boys gallop down from their rooms like an army in flight until we're all in the shelters underground. We're just standing around aimlessly while D.W. takes his own sweet time holding the phone to his ear as the warnings come through – purple, red, and so forth. For a solid hour, it's just "red" following "red." Tucked away in their shadowy nooks, the boys sing hymns; and every so often one of them sticks the tip of his nose out into the open. John and C. and I watch as the planes bore through the heavens unmolested and into the far distance. We step back inside. Presently, the "white" all-clear is given, and the boys bound triumphantly out of their hiding places. The lights come on, and everyone's face blushes. The boys work quietly until 8:30, then suppertime, which is louder tonight than ever. The place is full of whistling and singing until 9:45. The College horn sounds; we hold our short prayer service; and at 10:30, the last horn. Everyone to bed and "lights-out." There's a smattering of conversation here and there. Then, room-by-room, it stops. "Be quiet!" Nothing but a sea of silence until the bell strikes at seven in the morning.

October 21st: A day of thanksgiving – and a day of complete emptiness as well.[89] Why do I sense such barrenness today? There are only two empty days like this in town each year – excursion day for the Sunday School and this particular day of thanksgiving. So why do I feel like this? Because the shops are closed and the world has virtually come to a stop? They're also closed on Sundays, but Sundays don't feel the least bit empty to me. Maybe every day has its own work routine, its own rhythm, its own atmosphere. Isn't it because this routine is broken on thanksgiving day that a feeling of emptiness crops up?

As a way of trying to fill the void, I attend chapel service at seven this morning – the students' service. To my surprise, there are a hundred or more of our boys and girls here and a few other folks besides. It's a very special atmosphere, thanks in large measure to an incomparably fine morning sharpened by a hint of sacrifice and an aura of darkness. There are small candles in the chapel and many torches, like those in a Catholic Cathedral. Their light penetrates the darkness around them. And at this very same moment, the prayers of these students are penetrating the darkness as well. They penetrate and sparkle, they ignite and ascend – and defy the enveloping shadows. I wouldn't trade a prayer meeting like this one for a thousand others.

I head back to the house for breakfast with the children. Then to the College, and so forth for the rest of the day. In the evening, there's another prayer meeting; but I don't sense any of the expectant, profound atmosphere that was so palpable this morning. It does, however, conclude fervently with a prayerful shout. I almost feel like bear-hugging the preacher – because of the intensity of his passion and the purity of his Welsh. Such is the charisma of D.J.J.'s personality.

OCTOBER 24TH: It's the day of Porthaethwy Fair. The housegirl arrives at the crack of dawn, quite fraught and chattering a hot streak: "*Lord Haw-Haw*[90] said last night…that Hitler's air raid would be… targeting the Fair at eleven today."

"Who says so?"

"He does."

"Who's he?"

"Haw-Haw."

"How do you know?"

"Heard him."

"Who?"

"Him."

"You did?…with your own ears?…Are you sure?"

"Sure am, indeed!"

I head out to the College. She's true to her word! English airplanes are constantly darting about overhead – and it's hours before eleven. In addition, a great shouting noise rises up from the direction of Penmaenmawr. Even so, the road is bustling with horses and people making their way to the fair – a flood of them, in fact, is strolling across the bridge.

Eleven o'clock! The airplanes are still there, thousands by the look of them. And nothing else. Is *Haw-Haw* having his fun at our expense?

At one o'clock, I head home from the College. At that moment, the shrill sound of the Bangor air raid siren swells up into a long wail, sending a shiver of fright through the whole scene. Then the commotion begins…the panic…the scurrying about on foot and bicycle. Doors open and close. Commands bark as people are ordered off the roads and into their houses. The wardens turn out looking like proper giants under their hard hats while they strut half-boldly, half-sheepishly in the direction of town.

I reach the house. The children are all inside, frightened by the "Shriek of Bangor." Every one of them shows red eyes and traces of tears. In sympathy with the others, little Dewi has also been crying; and he's muttering something about the "hateful noise." The others are all talking bravely – now that I'm home!

Suddenly, there's a shout from somewhere that the danger has passed. And the children are back off to school, looking like heroes who've soldiered through fire and war! Dewi spends the entire afternoon talking about the "hateful noise," asking person after person – including all the residents on our street, as well as their dogs and cats! – if they too heard that "hateful noise."

And Porthaethwy Fair[91] manages to survive it all. Borne upon this little scrap of doggerel, its merriment reaches all the way to Bangor:

>...*A chwrw poeth o flaen y tân*
>*A geneth lân i'w charu.*
>[...A lusty beer before the fire
>And a lissome lass for loving.]

OCTOBER 27TH: Sunday. I'm off to Chapel in the morning. Today, it's Rev. Tom Nefyn Williams. His face looks like it's been carved from some precious, indestructible material and tempered afterwards by fire. His eyes are dove-like, and his demeanor and bearing are evangelical. With unmitigated earnestness, he asks: *"Who is my neighbor?"* It's a sermon full of vivid images – original, clever, apt.

In the afternoon, it's Sunday School. There are 18 in my class – impeccable students each one. They're somewhat fewer than on many Sundays; still, they account for more than three or four other classes taken together! Sunday School is wasting away everywhere you look. It's the nursery school of the church; and it's just, well, dying! Dying because of sin! Dying because of a general lack of effort to breathe new life into it. How easy it would be to transform Sunday School altogether. A bit of the old passion is what it craves – that's all! What if good folk expressed the same zeal for goodness that the wicked do for evil? What a difference that would make for the world and everything in it!

Back to Chapel in the evening. T.N.W.'s subject: "Seek first the Kindom of Heaven..." He starts off with illustrations, examples, readings and analogies. He seems to be swaying, floating, gliding – and it comes so naturally to him. He surges and sails. His intensity is subtly titillating, and he's borne upon a splendid stream as he strives towards his climax.[92] For several minutes – for quite a while, in fact, if you're marking time; but only for a moment in the experience – he strides the heights. Jesus, he declares: Is He the Object of our worship – the end? Or is He, is Jesus the Leader of our worship – the means? This preacher manages to have it both ways in the same hymn: "*I choose Jesus...*" He recites the entire thing, melodically. Then he sings it through, enchantingly. He thrills everyone. He electrifies everyone. He rivets every soul to his own without even seeming to breathe. There's no sense of time or place. No one else, nothing else exists. No one sees anything at all...except our preacher's immutable face. His voice is a torrent of appeals and declarations for and about Jesus – *for* our triumphal hopes, *about* our invincible convictions – that send us reeling in praise and joy. Here, undeniably, is a prophet. Here is a preacher at his blue best, a peerless exemplar of the Welsh pulpit at the pinnacle of eloquence.

After the service, the Membership confesses its faith and declares that it behooves everyone to stay a while longer yet – in consequence of such an outpouring of heavenly grace. No one dares move a step. Everyone stays put – we're all bound fast! We sing "*I choose Jesus...*" thrice over. Then we sing it again a thousand times more, each and every last one of us.

November the 1st: I'm going to hear Bob Owen[93] of Croesor speak at the College. He's lecturing on the subject of Wales' Contribution to the World. A satisfying subject, and well suited to such a mercurial character. He's a fellow-countryman who's bursting with facts; and his emotional fervor remains untamed by mere book-learning. His very skin seems to radiate holy enthusiasm, and his soul exudes brotherly kindness. He truly is a Welsh institution!

He's just flicked away his *Woodbine* [cigarette], and his hair is bristling. His tongue compels both head and body to do its bidding as his voice hoarsens and breaks – he's entirely at home on-stage. He's persuasive, provocative. He has this loud, mocking laugh. He insists; he threatens. He strides from one century to the next, from one continent to the next in but a single breath. There's no particular order, no real organization; he just gallops his way through an hour of time. It's all a heap of names, a string of facts, jumbled together higgledy-piggledy. This Gargantua tosses them out and handles them as his moods and whims dictate; meanwhile everyone shakes with laughter. What a patchwork-quilt of a lecture. What a masterpiece!

NOVEMBER 13TH: *Calangaeaf* [94] – the day all the folks out in the country set aside for telling stories about the old Spirits.

It's also Lowri's birthday. Eight years old? That's just incredible! I can remember the day she was born like it was yesterday – that marvelous Sunday. There was a glow in the air, an even warmer one in my heart. The gentleness of the moment, the quietness of the fields – those were my boon companions on that particular day.

Eight years. They've gone by like minutes. But to Lowri, they seem like mountains of time; and she's been longing for this birthday for what has seemed an age of ages. And *today*, it's all about her – until teatime, that is, when she's already starting to think about next year's birthday. She's been awfully full of herself today, but she hasn't run wild like the twins did on their birthday. For her gift we give her the book *Tylwyth Teg* [*The Fairy Family*] by Huw Evans. At teatime, it's a cake, as usual, but without icing this go-round, since sugar is so scarce. Chocolate does the trick instead; and there are eight candles, of course. It gets dark after tea, so I pull out the magic lantern [i.e., slide projector] and show some pictures while Luned reads aloud a story from *Y Fantell Fraith* [*The Calico Cloak*] by Hooson.[95] Everyone's fantasizing and daydreaming – and deploring their luck when it all comes to an end.

Enough bliss for one day, I suppose.

DECEMBER 12TH: What a fine morning – the first we've had like this for weeks. The sun is smiling on me as I head to the College, and the image of white clouds running after it makes for a beautiful scene.

Luned is talking about going to Llandudno, not for a seaside vacation but to go Christmas shopping for the children and everybody else besides. There are virtually no children's toys of any sort in the Bangor shops – except very precious ones at exorbitant prices, that is. Even chocolate is impossible to find.

She returns to the house soon after tea with rather a full load. We'll have to hide everything in a *"cwat tlws"*[96] somewhere out of view of the children. It wouldn't pay for them to know who *Siôn Corn*[97] really is!

DECEMBER 18TH: The end of term is approaching. I'm supervising examinations instead of lecturing. It takes two hours this first morning; and the students are hard at it, concentrating with all their might. The scene is energetic, full of exertion that verges on genuine devotion. Examinations reign supreme; and self-commitment conquers all – if only for this brief fraction of time!

I make my way home to grade 150 papers, in only two or three days! I realize how unfair and incomplete my evaluations really are.

Still, I keep at it until evening – until I'm just too tired, in both body and soul. I grab a copy of *Y Faner*, and I read it through. S.L. [Saunders Lewis] is very good on the subject of *Where the World is Heading*.

DECEMBER 21ST:[98] I've finished marking all my papers, so from now on it's the holidays! I spend the morning in the house. I'm reading *The Last Days of Paris* by Alexander Werth.[99] It's a diary as well (must be a trend). Good descriptions – succinct, lively, moving, raw – of what happened in May, June and July in France. Every sentence is gripping and sticks with you. Some will pierce you to the quick or give you the shivers. The diary itself is far superior to its *epilogue* – Charles d'Ydewalle[100] or J. Bainville, were he still alive, should have been persuaded to write that.

There's one other fault: I detect at least a hint or two of an Englishman's self-righteousness. From his lofty perch, Werth – this Englishman – is inclined to look down upon the French; and he half-winces, mockingly, at their trials and tribulations and distress. It's unpardonable! True enough, the author loves France in his own way – but on condition, perhaps, that France must return that love and suffer for England, even fight England's battles! The France he knows is Official France, the France of politicians, of coteries of dwarves and refuse pits of corruption. But this isn't the *true, un*official France that even today remains undefiled by the rabble of sorry creatures who constitute the Third Republic.

In spite of everything, I enjoy the book.

DECEMBER 25TH: Christmas! The miracles of its comforting, joyful atmosphere have been manifesting themselves for days, despite the war. The lightheartedness that is a hallmark of the season fills the air. Late last night, I pulled down three books to enjoy on this happy day – *Lettres de mon moulin* [*Letters from my Windmill*],[101] *Mon* oncle et mon curé [*My Uncle and my Curate*]¹⁰² and *Le foyer Breton* [*The Breton Foyer*].¹⁰³ At the same time, Luned retrieved the children's gifts from their hiding place and arranged them on the kitchen hearth. She also filled their five stockings while they quietly slept. Then, we went to bed ourselves.

And now, it's between six and seven in the morning. The twins, as usual, wake up first. They're out of bed and down the stairs – like mice! They're in the kitchen. (Luned hears every peep, every word.) Gasps of surprise lead to whispering, and whispering leads to talking:

"Oh, look!" Mererid says, "a little basket – a green one, just like I wanted. Oh my!"

"And a motor car for me!" Hywel exclaims. "Look there!" They've seen the stockings and rush at them, shouting in unison, "Candy, and chocolate, and nuts, and books…"

Next, Lowri awakens and hears all the merriment. She leaps up and makes for the kitchen. "Oh! A knitting bag!" There's a pregnant pause, then a shout: "Oh, and there's a sewing bag in there too…and a thimble…small scissors…and a measuring tape and needles. My own books too!"

It's serious business now – they're consumed with unwrapping, unboxing, rummaging, making a fuss. The children keep trying to attract each other's attention, and they're all showing off their Welsh books. Finally, they're persuaded to return to bed for a spell. And, if you can believe it, they go! – taking handfuls of sweets and nuts with them, which they nibble as fast as they can. Curiously enough, Dewi has slept through the whole hullaballoo. So Luned takes him by the arm, and they go downstairs together: his goodies lie undisturbed on the hearth beside all the others'.

"Look here, Dewi!"

"Yes, puff-puff, and puff-puff smoke!"

"Who brought them?" Luned asks.

"*Siôn Corn* brought them…for Dai…and a little…tiny motor car. And lots of pencils for little Dai."

(For some time now, it's Dai, not Dewi, that he's wanted us to call him.)

• • • • •

So that's how our day started. The children ate breakfast at a gallop, then skipped into another room to spend hours with all the toys that *Siôn Corn* left for them during his journey from chimney to chimney. They were on their knees and bellies all morning long. Tom Parry stopped by. What a commotion! In all the confused excitement, it must have seemed that everyone was prostrate on the floor. It was probably enough to frighten Tom out of raising a family of his own.

A little while after dinner, the children headed out to the Cathedral to look at the small replica of Bethlehem, with its stable, the Star above and Mary and Joseph with the Baby in the manger. Outside, there were shepherds and wise men, even camels. The little ones were spellbound, and that's all they could talk about at teatime.

Before calling it a day, we sat around the fire and sang carols and hymns together. Then, to bed – after about as much playing and laughing and carrying-on as body and soul can take. Here and there, during lulls between the noise, I managed to read *Mon oncle et mon curé* with as much satisfaction as ever. To each his own heaven on Christmas Day! Even during war, which has seemed to enjoy its own version of Christmas Day respite. The weather saw to it that there'd be no war in the air. May the weather be blessed, then, for restoring God's splendid old idea of "Peace on Earth" during the holiday season. Let me commend You for Your wisdom, then. Yours is the only wisdom anywhere to be found amidst the darkness of a world that has lost its God.

December 31st: The last day of the year, 1940! Today, you finally come to an end; and you are draped in the purple shroud of slaughter – just like Efnisien with that cauldron over in Ireland.[104] You come to an end, and so do your daily papers full of horrible news – such as, for instance, the devastation visited upon London only last Saturday night. You will end in destruction, in fire. At last, you will end! It will end! May it end – *please*!

• • • • •

I'm the one who'll write your memoir. How tame, how pale it will be compared with your rabid fury. Let the fury come to an end as well! So we can forget you and your rapacious passions. Instead, we'll warm our hearts basking in the humane and benevolent tenderness of Alphonse Daudet and his *Lettres*.

The children are jumping for joy at a *parti*. It's an end-of-the-year celebration at the home of one of their pals – Goronwy Owen[105] by name, if you can believe that! And he's one of the liveliest little peppercorns you ever saw. In the midst of their shenanigans, I have to bring them back home, to their great annoyance of course. This last evening of the year is calling for its ominous, dark shadows to enfold us – even while wayfarers here and there shout, "Happy New Year!" as they pass us by.

Epilogue

(Having just read the entire preceding draft, Luned has this to say:)

"Usually I think of you as, well, fairly unassuming. But now? This…this is just so *selfish*. You've really gone overboard this time!"

"Give me one example."

"One example? There's no *one* example. There are dozens of them! Look at this…and this…and this…"

I disagree *vehemently*, of course – for a moment anyway. Then, I suppose I have to agree with her, if not vehemently then at least grudgingly – and most contritely as well.

A diary? Why, the very premise of a diary is selfishness itself – even more so the decision to publish one.

"He hides my sins from the people."[106]

Notes to 1940: Gleanings from a Diary

1. *Heb flew ar ei dafod*; literally, "without hairs on his tongue."
2. *A'n gwynt yn ein dwrn*; literally, "with our wind in our fist."
3. Two brothers, Aneirin ap Talfan and Alun T. Davies, M.A., LL.B., were the founders and editors of *Llyfrau'r Dryw* [Wren Press], today known as Christopher Davies Ltd. Aneirin (1909-80) also served as Head of Programmes for BBC Wales for a period beginning in 1966.
4. *Dydd-lyfr pythefnos, neu dawns angau* [*A Fortnight's Diary, or a Dance of Death*] (1939), in which the author documents his last two weeks in France and Brittany before the outbreak of World War II.
5. The Old New Year [i.e. according to the Julian-calendar]; or 14 January 1941.
6. Bebb was one of the forefathers of political Welsh nationalism and co-founder with Saunders Lewis and others in 1924 of *Y Mudiad Cymreig* [The Welsh Movement, forerunner of *Plaid Cymru*, the present-day Party of Wales]. He formally broke with his colleagues in 1939 over his party's insistence on Welsh neutrality and pacifism in the face of what Bebb perceived was the dire threat of Hitler's adventurism.
7. 1914: The Great War/World War I; 1911: Germany's fierce protest of French intervention in the "Fez Crisis" in Morocco; 1870: "Franco-Prussian War"; 1814: Napoleon's "Defence of France" against the Allies, led by Prussia.

8. Johann Wolfgang von Goethe commented on this very subject in a conversation recorded by Johann Peter Eckermann, 23 October 1828. What follows is a representative excerpt: "Frankfurt, Bremen, Hamburg, Luebeck are large and brilliant, and their impact on the prosperity of Germany is incalculable. Yet, would they remain what they are if they were to lose their independence and be incorporated as provincial cities into one great German Empire? I have reason to doubt this."

9. All are writers who treated various aspects of French and Breton nationalism.

10. Wife of the author.

11. The "Fairy Family" of Welsh legend, said to inhabit the slopes of Newydd Fynyddog (near Llanidloes).

12. Instead of *"yn enw'r Tad"* [in the name of the Father].

13. Conscientious Objector.

14. Fransez Debauvais and Olier Mordrel, co-founders of the Breton Nationalist Party in 1931.

15. *Die Kultur der Renaissance in Italien* (1860) by Jacob Burckhardt; *The Civilization of the Renaissance in Italy* (English translation, 1878).

16. Paris, 1933.

17. At the Battle of Suomussalmi (7 Dec. 1939-8 Jan. 1940) Finnish forces under Marshal Baron Carl von Mannerheim repelled the invading Russian Red Army. Against 27,500 Russians killed or frozen to death, the Finns suffered but 900 killed, 1,770 wounded.

18. One shilling/three pence; roughly equivalent to £2.35 or $3.75 today.

19. See note 6 above.

20. A reference to Jesus at the Mount of Olives, after the Last Supper. See Matthew 26:39: "And [Jesus] went a little farther, and fell on his face, and prayed, saying, 'O my Father, if it be possible, let this cup pass from me: nevertheless not as I will, but as thou wilt.'"

21. "Leap Day," 1940.

22. *Baner ac Amserau Cymru* [*Banner and Times of Wales*], weekly newspaper founded in 1859.

23. Published 1939; translated into English by M. K. Stengel (publication pending).

24 Paper rationing on account of the war required a significant shortening of Bebb's submitted manuscript. Eventually, the author would publish most of this eliminated material in 1951 as *Machlud yr Oesoedd Canol: Hanes Cymru ar Ddiwedd yr Oesoedd Canol* [*Twilight of the Middle Ages: A History of Wales at the End of the Medieval Period*]. In 1995, the late Sir R.R. Davies described this latter work as "a charming and undervalued portrait of Welsh society based on the evidence of the poetry [of the period]." It too has been translated into English by M. K. Stengel (publication pending).

25 *Digon o waith*; literally, "because enough."

26 Célestin Lainé (1908-1983), radical, and violent Breton nationalist who collaborated with the Nazi occupiers of France in hopes of establishing an independent Brittany. He died in exile in Ireland.

27 "Brittany House," in Breton, followed by Welsh translation.

28 "*Standing Upright*," in Breton.

29 Deiniolen, near the slate quarry at Dinorwic, was often called Llanbabo on account of the quarrymen working there who hailed from the Anglesey village of the same name.

30 Excerpt from the title poem of the volume *Terfysgoedd Daear* [*Earth's Tumults*] (1939), by the Welsh Radical poet and Marxist labor champion T.E. Nicholas ["Niclas y Glais"], 1878-1971.

31 In English.

32 A subtle insinuation is here implied: From a pan-Celtic point of view, French dominion over Brittany is analogous with English dominion over Wales. By suggesting that Bebb now sympathizes with France, S. Lewis as much as accuses his erstwhile colleague of championing the oppressor over the oppressed.

33 Mid- to late 14th century; late 15th century & early 16th century; and mid- to late 15th century, respectively. (See note 24 above.)

34 G.R. Owst, *Literature and Pulpit in Medieval England* (1934).

35 The opening words of a well known anonymous poem in the style of the celebrated 14th-century bard Dafydd ap Gwilym: *Pan ddel Mai a'i lifrai las/ ar irddail i roi'r urddas,/ aur a dyf ar edafedd/ ar y llwyn er mwyn a'i medd.* [When May comes in its green livery/ with ordination for the fresh leaves,/ then gold grows along the threads/ of the bush for him who owns it. – translation by Gwyn Williams, in *An Introduction to Welsh Poetry* (1970)].

36 The beginning of May (with *Calan Mai*, or May Day) is not necessarily the first day of May, as is often supposed. Instead, actual May Day signifies the "cross-quarter day" between vernal equinox and summer solstice, according to ancient Celtic calendar customs. Considered the arrival of summer, this time of year was celebrated with the bonfire festival known as *Beltane* ["*tân*" being Welsh for "fire"].

37 Modern-day Palestine.

38 A native of Cardiganshire in rural West Wales.

39 In Celtic legend, the otherworldly Land of Eternal Youth.

40 Douglas Hyde (1860-1949), Irish bard and folklorist, and first President of the Irish Republic, 1938-1945; Éamon de Valera (1882-1975), Irish Republican statesman, and the first *taoiseach* or prime minister of the Irish Republic (1937-48, and subsequently 1951-54 and 1957-59) as well as the Republic's third president (1959-73).

41 Cf., Psalm 23:5–"Thou preparest a table before me in the presence of mine enemies: thou anointest my head with oil; my cup runneth over."

42 Cereal grains, in general, are referred to as "corn" in Wales and England; Indian (American) "corn" is referred to as "maize."

43 (Henri) Phillippe (Omer) Pétain (1856-1951), hero of the Battle of Verdun (1916), was elevated to commander-in-chief (*Maréchal*) of French forces in 1917. After the defeat of France in 1940, Pétain collaborated with the Germans, who confirmed his authority over the rump state of Vichy France. He died while imprisoned after the commutation of his post-war death sentence for treason against France.

44 These questions all refer to the Germans' "Drive to the Channel," 16-21 May 1940: After French General Maurice G. Gamelin hesitated too long to call up France's reserves, he was relieved as Allied commander by General Maxime Weygand on 19 May. Nevertheless, German Panzers reached the coast west of Abbeville, isolating the British Expeditionary Force – which soon made good a desperate evacuation from beaches at Dunkirk, 28 May-4 June.

45 *Pa ddrwg sydd yn y caws?*; literally, "What's wrong with the cheese?"

46 The armored tanks and aircraft of the German *blitzkrieg*.

⁴⁷ [From the Breton:] "Hallo! Hallo, Comrades. Here's some good news for you. Everybody listen: Radio Brittany will bring you the news every night between eight p.m. and a quarter-past." –*W.A. Bebb*

⁴⁸ In 1859, with France as its ally, the Italian Piedmont defied Austria in the cause of Italian independence, which ultimately was achieved under the Piedmontese King Victor Emmanuel II.

⁴⁹ All were influential French statesmen of the late 19th/early 20th centuries: (Louis) Adolphe Thiers (1797-1877); Léon Michel Gambetta (1838-1882); Raymond Nicolas Landry Poincaré (1860-1934); Georges Eugène Benjamin Clemençeau (1841-1929).

⁵⁰ All were French writers, royalists and nationalist agitators: Charles Maurras (1868-1952), convicted as a Vichy collaborator in 1945; Jacques Bainville (1879-1936); Léon Daudet (1867-1942).

⁵¹ Most likely, Bwlan Calvinist Methodist chapel in Llandwrog.

⁵² *Lleu* means "light, brightness." The author intends, in this instance, for Dinas Dinlleu to be understood as the City of the Fortress of Light, an allusion no doubt to Paris' own renown as the City of Light. Dinas Dinlleu is an Iron Age hill fort 10 miles south of Caern*arfon* (at Nantlle). Its name actually refers to the legendary Welsh hero of the Mabinogion myth-cycle, Lleu Llaw Gyffes, whose fortress-home this is said to be. In a further (deliberate) irony, *Lleu* is considered a Welsh adaptation of *Lug*, the Gaulish god of light and the sun. (Even at Chapel, it seems, the Celtic Otherworld and Welsh pre-history are never far off.)

⁵³ (Arthur) Neville Chamberlain (1869-1940), British prime minister 1937-1940; Stanley Baldwin, 1st Earl of Bewdley (1867-1947), prime minister 1923-1924, 1924-1929 and 1935-1937; (James) Ramsay MacDonald (1866-1937), prime minister 1924, 1929-1935.

⁵⁴ In English

⁵⁵ *Gwifrau barfog*; literally, "bearded wires." (Note that, in English, "barb" ultimately derives, as well, from the Latin *barba*, "beard.")

⁵⁶ The summer solstice, Midsummer's Day.

⁵⁷ By capitulating to German terms, the French were abruptly spurning Winston Churchill's offer of an "indissoluble union" by which Franco-English forces would carry on the war effort jointly and indefinitely from bases in North Africa.

[58] *"ac y mae golwg sobr a syn ar weddill bob amser, megis..."*; source of quotation is obscure.

[59] *"Stafell Gynddylan, ys tywyll heno..."*; first line of a famous Welsh poem, by an anonymous bard, lamenting the fallen 7th-century king Cynddylan, now scarcely remembered.

[60] A typographical omission in the original has resulted in an uncertain date for this passage.

[61] Giuseppe Mazzini (1805-1872), Italian nationalist and republican agitator, was first exiled to then expelled from France in the 1830s.

[62] A French equivalent for "and so on, and so forth; etc., etc." – a mocking pun on the name Pétain, perhaps?

[63] In June 1940, General Charles de Gaulle escaped to England and set about organizing the Free French forces, later known as *La Résistance*.

[64] At Oran Harbor, Algeria, a British squadron demanded that France put its North African fleet beyond the grasp of the Germans. When France refused, the English opened fire, and three French battleships were sunk. A similar ultimatum at Alexandria resulted in the voluntary disarming of the French squadron there. Pétain, furious, severed diplomatic relations between his Vichy government and that of Great Britain on 5 July.

[65] From personal correspondence with Mr. Ifan Bebb, youngest son of the author: "I understand that Sir Artemus Jones defended Sir Roger Casement in 1916, when the more senior barrister [Sergeant A.M. Sullivan] was unable to carry on. He has another claim to fame with regard to Libel Laws. I remember his widow in Twrgwyn Chapel when I was a child." [Sir Roger Casement, who sought German assistance in achieving Irish independence during World War I, was hanged for high treason in England, 1916.]

[66] Members of *Plaid Cymry*, the Party of Wales.

[67] A reference to D.R. Hughes perhaps, a notable Welsh essayist of the period.

[68] I.e., traitors, *agents provocateurs*; an expression attributed to General Mola during the Spanish Civil War (1936-9), who boasted of surrounding Madrid with four columns of the army, while a fifth one intrigued on his behalf inside the city itself.

[69] Spoken in English.

Glimpses of Life in Wales

70 A Miss Hughes and Mr. Edward Bebb Hughes, already introduced in the author's foreword to his great-great-uncle's diary from 1841. Titled *Y Baradwys Bell* [*The Faraway Paradise*], its English translation constitutes the first half of the present work.

71 William Rees ("Gwilym Hiraethog"; 1802-1883), writer and abolitionist.

72 Verse-forms known in Welsh as *pennillion*.

73 *The Silk Dress* (1939), a novel by Elena Puw Morgan (1900-1973).

74 Plas Iolyn, a half-mile to the west of the village of Rhydlydan near Betws-y-Coed, was the manor house of Elis Prys, "the Red Doctor" (1512?-1594?), a Tudor-era Parliamentarian and official who was instrumental in the Dissolution of the Monasteries. Upon his death, the manor passed to his son Tomos (*c.* 1564-1634), an accomplished soldier-poet (said to be the first person to smoke tobacco publicly in London).

75 A reference, perhaps, to Alun Roberts, educator and fellow faculty member with the author at the Normal College, Bangor.

76 "Oat Field," "Wheat Field" and "Fallow Field," respectively.

77 Note that the former phrase, *Get-Ws*, is a phonetic-Welsh approximation of the English original. The latter, *Tŷ'n y Porth*, is proper Welsh: literally, House in the Gate.

78 The child uses "shortcut English" for his number; in Welsh numeracy, 24 is expressed, literally, as "four on twenty."

79 "Shortcut English" again; in Welsh, 67 is *saith ar drigain* (seven on three twenties).

80 The author's 46th. According to Bebb's biographer Robin Chapman, Bebb's birth certificate indicated a date of 7 July 1894, although the author himself considered this an error.

81 Literally, "Owain, son of Ambrose Bebb."

82 Owain Gwynedd, or Owain ap Gruffudd (*c.* 1100-1170), powerful Welsh ruler and statesman. He acknowledged the overlordship of Henry II of England but styled himself Prince (*Y Llyw*) over the other lordships of Wales. He and his descendants, ending with Llywelyn ap Gruffudd, *Y Llyw Olaf* [The Last Prince] (*c.* 1225-1282) thus constituted the one and only dynasty of native Princes of Wales.

83 According to the author in the preceding work, "*wtra*" is a distinctive Montgomeryshire colloquialism. (See note 34 page 75.)

A Welsh Hundred

84 The German invasion of Poland, 1-5 September 1939; considered the opening hostilities of World War II.

85 A *stacan* [plural, *stacanau*] is four or six sheaves that have been stood up against one another. In Montgomeryshire, they're referred to as "*bwch*" [plural, *bychod*]. –W.A. Bebb

86 An open cart with a pole at every corner, used to gather hay and grain. –W.A. Bebb

87 Before the war, Shire School curricula were oriented towards academic studies and university preparation; Middle Schools were more concerned with teaching general and technical subjects.

88 Bethesda, in the heart of North Wales' slate-quarrying district, is famed for its many Nonconformist chapels.

89 Trafalgar Day celebrates the victory at sea, on 21 October 1805, of Vice-Admiral Horatio Nelson over the combined navies of France and Spain. After WWI, observations of Trafalgar Day with its inherent triumphalism gradually waned, only to be superseded by the more somber observances of Remembrance Day each 11 November commemorating the 1918 armistice that ended the slaughter of "The Great War."

90 William Joyce (1906-1946), British Fascist and Nazi propagandist of Anglo-Irish descent who broadcast in English from Germany. He was hanged for treason after the war.

91 *Ffair y Borth*, or Porthaethwy Fair, is held annually on 24 October and dates to 1691.

92 Here is a classic rendition of religious *hwyl*, whose untranslatable yet ecstatic intensity represents perhaps the supreme achievement of Welsh Chapel Culture.

93 Robert Owen (1885-1962), antiquary, book-collector and genealogist with particular expertise on the subject of Welsh emigration.

94 The old Celtic "New Year," ancient designation for the first day of winter (*gaeaf*).

95 I.D. (Isaac Daniel) Hooson (1880-1948); *Y Fantell Fraith* is his 1934 adaptation of Robert Browning's "The Pied Piper of Hamelin."

96 Literally, "lair for jewels" – a hiding place.

97 "John of the Horn (o'plenty)"; i.e., Father Christmas.

98 Winter solstice, shortest day of the year.

[99] Alexander Werth (1901-1969), Russian-born, naturalized British writer and journalist. This book is subtitled, "A Journalist's Diary."

[100] Belgian writer and journalist (1901-1985).

[101] By Alphonse Daudet (1840-1897), father of Léon Daudet, *op. cit.*, note 50 above. *Lettres de mon moulin* was published in 1869.

[102] By Jean de la Brète, pseudonym of Alice Cherbonnel (1858-1945). *Mon oncle et mon curé* was published in 1889.

[103] By Emile Souvestre (1806-1854). *Le foyer Breton* was published in 1845.

[104] Efnisien, a Welsh character in the "Second Branch" of the Mabinogion myth-cycle, aids his countrymen during their battle against the Irish by shattering the *Pair Dadeni* [Cauldron of Rebirth], in which the Irish war dead were previously able to restore themselves to life. While accomplishing this feat, however, Efnisien was himself destroyed.

[105] The boy's namesake, Goronwy Owen (*Goronwy Ddu o Fôn*) (1723-1769) was perhaps the greatest Welsh bard of the 18th century. He emigrated to America, where he died and was buried in Virginia.

[106] "*Cudd fy meiau rhag y werin.*" From the hymn *Syllu ar Galfaria* [Gazing upon Calvary] by the Rev. William Williams of Pantycelyn; published 1840.

Index

A

Action Française xxiv
Agrarian Movement xvi, xvii, xix, xxi, xxiv, xxvi
Anti-loving-in-the-bed Society 21

B

Bainville, Jacques 127, 163, 173
Baldwin, Stanley 129, 173
Bebb, Edward 10, 75, 175
Bebb family homesteads
  Cilwinllan 10, 12, 13, 20, 22, 33, 34, 75, 80, 139, 146, 147
  Rhiwgriafol 11, 12, 13, 17, 22, 23
  Tawelan 12
Bebb family (W.A.)
  Dewi xxxvii, 20, 23, 76, 93, 98, 106, 109, 120, 124, 127, 131, 132, 145, 146, 148, 158, 159, 164, 165
  Enid 79, 124, 127, 131
  Hywel xxxvii, 85, 93, 106, 128, 148, 164
  Lowri xxxvii, 75, 93, 106, 139, 143, 146, 148, 161, 164
  Luned 93, 97, 105, 107, 120, 123, 124, 127, 132, 145, 146, 148, 150, 162, 164, 165, 167
  Mererid xxxvii, 85, 93, 106, 128, 148, 164
  Owain 145

A Welsh Hundred

Bebb family (Wm.)
  Margiad 29
  Margiad (daughter) 29, 34
  Margiad (wife) 29, 34
Bebb, W. Ambrose xi, xv, xx, xxv, xxix, xxx, xxxi, xxxiii, xxxiv, 1, 3, 14, 79, 81, 90, 175, 189
  works xii, xiii, xiv, xv, xxi, xxiv, xxxiii, xxxiv, xxxv, 3, 97, 102, 107, 113, 118, 131, 169, 170, 171, 172, 174, 190
Bebb, William (in America) 17, 33, 55, 67, 73, 75, 76, 79
Bebb, William (in Wales) xiii, xv, 10, 11, 14, 17, 70, 79
Beer Act of 1830 26
Belgium 118, 121
Blitzkrieg 118, 172
Breese, John 13
Breton publications
  Breiz Atao [Brittany Forever] 189
  Ouest-Informations [West-Intelligencer] 104, 123
  Sav [Standing Upright] 104
British Parliament 189
Brittany xiv, xix, xxi, xxvii, 34, 91, 92, 96, 97, 104, 105, 107, 115, 116, 131, 135, 146, 169, 171, 173, 189, 190
  Lorient 133
  Morlaix 133
  Quimper 104, 133
  Rennes xiv, 104, 131, 133
Brittany House (Ker Vreiz) 104
Burckhardt, Jacob 96, 170

C

Canada 45
Chamberlain, (Arthur) Neville 129, 173
Chapman, Robin xvi, xxxiii, xxxiv, xxxv, 175
Chartism xv, 18, 19, 21, 31, 74
Cherbonnel, Alice (Jean de la Brète) 164, 165, 177
Clemençeau, Georges Eugène Benjamin 126, 173
Coal pits 36
Colin, Joseph Marie 104
Conscientious objectors 94, 117, 139
Corn Laws (Corn Duty) 64

D

Dafydd ap Gwilym 108, 171
Daniel, J.E. xxxvi
Daudet, Alphonse 93, 163, 166, 177
Daudet, Léon 127
Davies, D. Hywel xxv, xxxv
Davies, Sir Rees R. xii
Davies, Walter (Gwallter Mechain) 9, 28, 31, 49, 51, 76
Davis, David (the Rascal) 49, 52, 60
Debauvais, Fransez 95, 104, 117, 123, 135, 170
Denmark 108

E

Edward, prince of Wales (later, Edward VII) 41, 63
Edwards, Lewis 27, 50
Edwards, Roger 38
Edwards, Sir John 58
Efnisien (and the Cauldron of Rebirth) 166, 177
Elias, John 9, 18, 19, 20, 21, 26, 27, 32, 38, 41, 44, 45, 46, 47, 48, 54, 57, 73, 74, 78
England xxiii, xxvi, xxxv, 16, 28, 66, 92, 95, 98, 107, 111, 133, 134, 137, 144, 163, 171, 172, 174, 175
  London xxvii, xxxv, 18, 24, 31, 40, 79, 93, 95, 102, 103, 113, 166, 175
  Shrewsbury 13
Enlightened despotism 111

F

Finland, Battle for 103, 170
France xxi, 91, 104, 105, 107, 111, 113, 114, 117, 118, 120, 121, 122, 123, 124, 126, 128, 132, 133, 134, 135, 137, 163, 169, 171, 172, 173, 174, 176, 189
  Dijon 133
  Limoges 133
  Lyon 133
  Nantes 133
  Paris xiv, xxi, 104, 109, 125, 126, 163, 170, 173, 189
  St. Malo 133
Frost, John 74

G

Gambetta, Léon Michel 126, 134, 173
Germany xxi, xxv, 92, 98, 124, 132, 134, 169, 170, 176
  Berlin xxiv, xxvii, xxxv, 123, 154
Goethe, Johann Wolfgang von 92, 170

H

Harvest-time xv, 33, 39, 49, 54, 55, 60, 79, 80, 89, 147, 148
Heine, Heinrich 92
Hen Gorff, Y ["The Old Body"] 13, 17, 31, 54, 73, 74, 129, 173
Herrieu, Loeiz 131, 133, 135
Hitler, Adolf xxv, 98, 104, 108, 113, 135, 157, 169
Hooson, Isaac Daniel 162, 176
Howell, William 41, 78
Hughes, Edward Bebb 10, 175
Hughes, John 38
Hughes, Richard 16, 22
Hughes, Tomas 34, 35
Hughes, William Bebb 10
Humphreys, Morgan 138
Hyde, Douglas 115, 172

I

Idioms and sayings xiii, 17, 21, 23, 24, 25, 26, 27, 30, 31, 32, 39, 43, 54, 61, 62, 69, 77, 83, 93, 98, 102, 106, 113, 115, 121, 134, 139, 146, 161, 162, 167, 171, 175
Ifans, Robert 34
Iron works 36
Italy xvii, 122, 124, 134, 170
  Rome xxi, 27, 124
Ivorites 32

J

Jackson, Andrew (U.S. president) 66
Jarman, Risiart 40
Jones, Artemus 138, 174
Jones, Charles 40
Jones, Evan 14, 73
Jones, Gwynn 115
Jones, John 9, 19, 20, 73

Jones, William 29, 74
Joyce, William ("Lord Haw-Haw") 157

L

Lainé, Célestin 104, 171
Le Braz, Anatole 93
Leopold, King of Belgium 121
Le Rouzic, Zacharie 105
Lewis, Saunders xiv, xv, xxxiii, 102, 107, 163, 169
Lime, for soil conditioning 12, 34, 43
Lloyd, Roger Bradshaigh 103

M

MacDonald, (James) Ramsay 129, 173
Madog ap Owain Gwynedd 28
Madogwys Indians 28
Maurras, Charles xxiv, xxv, 127, 135, 173
Mazzini, Guiseppe 134, 174
Medieval studies 77, 96, 108, 171, 190
Monetary values 18, 20, 97
Mordrel, Olier 96, 117, 123, 135, 170
Morgan, Dafydd 38
Mostyn family 19, 106
Mussolini, Benito xxiv, 104, 122

N

Nashville, Tenn. xvi, xxxii, xxxviii, 191
National Library of Wales 115
National Party of Brittany 95
New Poor Laws of 1834 21, 22, 33, 35, 42, 70, 74
New York 40, 66
Nicholas, T.E. ("Niclas y Glais") 171
Nonconformism (also, see Religious denominations) 76, 176
Nordström, Johan 96
Norway, Battle for 108, 109

O

Oddfellows 32, 39
Ohio
 Ebensburgh 16, 22, 23

    Hamilton 55
    Harding 65
    Lima 64
    Ottawa 64
    Van Wert 64, 65, 70
Owen, David 20, 23, 76
Owen, Robert 160

P

Peel, Sir Robert 57, 79
Péguy 93
Pétain, Henri Phillippe Omer 118
Picquenard, C.A. 105
Poincaré, Raymond Nicholas Landry 126, 173
Poor house 22
Powell, Thomas 40
Price, Tomas (Carhuanawc) 28
Prys, Elis ("the Red Doctor") 141, 143, 175
Prys, Thomas 141

R

Ransom, John Crowe xix, xx, xxxiv
Rechabites, Independent Order of 49
Rees, William ("Gwilym Hiraethog") 141
Rees, William (Gwilym Hiraethog) 9, 175
Reform Bill of 1832 15, 74
Religious denominations
  Anabaptists 17
  Baptists 64
  Calvinistic Methodism 13, 17, 31, 54, 73, 74, 129, 173
  Calvinistic Methodists 12, 32, 76
  Campbellites 17
  Independent-Congregationalists 28, 64
  Roman Catholics 17, 29, 34, 67, 73, 74
Renaissance studies xvii, 96, 122, 170
Richards, Thomas 31
Roberts, John 13, 25, 39, 66, 74, 75
Roberts, Samuel 9, 39, 56, 73, 76, 78, 79, 80
Rolland, Charles 105
Rules for a household 36

S

Siôn Corn (Father Christmas) 162, 165
Socialism 107
Souvestre, Emile 93, 164, 177
Stalin, Joseph 97
Storms and tempests xv, 30, 65, 67
Sunday School 17, 27, 36, 53, 58, 127, 156, 159

T

Tate, Allen xx, xxi, xxiii, xxiv, xxxiv, xxxv
Temperance Movement (The Cause) 12, 19, 20, 26, 29, 34, 35, 38, 45, 46, 49, 67
Thiers, (Louis) Adolphe 126, 134, 173
Tir Na'n Og (Irish Land of Eternal Youth) 115
Transportation (the Royal Mercy) 18, 31, 41, 74
Treaty of Versailles 92
Tylwyth Teg (the Fairy Family) 62, 93, 161

V

Vanderbilt University xvi, xxiii, xxxviii
Victoria, Queen of England 63

W

Watcyn Wyn family 19, 41, 42, 43
Welsh Assembly xvi
Welsh bards (Medieval & Renaissance) 108, 113, 171
Welsh language, obstacles to xv, 28, 77, 103, 111, 123, 144, 150
Welsh Language Society 18, 20, 24
Welsh Movement, The xvi, 169
Welsh Nationalist Party xvi, xvii, xix, xx, xxv, xxvii, xxxv, 169, 170, 189
Welsh places
  Aberglaslyn Bridge 114, 146
  Anglesey 21, 26, 29, 47, 102, 110, 139, 171
  Aran Fawddwy iii, 11, 140
  Bont Dolgadfan 12
  Breconshire 73, 76, 155
  Cader Idris 11, 24, 25, 60
  Caernarfonshire 25, 92, 102, 129
  Carneddi Range 150
  Cors Caron xv

Cwmbychan 95
Cyfeiliog 16
Deheubarth 10
Denbighshire 20, 73, 137
Dinas Dinlleu 129, 173
Glamorgan 68
Gwynedd 10, 41, 76, 145, 175
Lake Eiddwen xiv
Llanberis Lake 105
Llanfair Talhaearn 12
Llanidloes 12, 18, 26, 29, 32, 34, 36, 40, 49, 62, 170
Llanwyddelan 12
Llechwedd Isaf 150
Menai Strait 46, 47, 156
Moelfre 12
Monmouth 68, 155
Newydd Fynyddog 62, 170
Pen Mynydd 141
Penrhyn 141, 144
Pentre Ariannel 141
Plas Iolyn 141, 142, 175
Powys xxxvii, 10, 31, 41, 48
Pumlumon xiv, 11
Radnorshire 155
Taff Vale 48
Tal-y-llyn 146
Taren y Gesail 11
Vale of Maentwrog 114
Y Faenol 142
Y Gesail Gyfarch 141
Yr Wyddfa [Mount Snowdon] 105, 114

Welsh publications
- Athraw [The Tutor] 27
- Baner ac Amserau Cymru [The Banner and Times of Wales], also Y Faner [The Banner] 75, 163, 189
- Dirwestwr [Temperance-man] 27, 67
- Drysorfa [Treasury] 27, 32, 50
- Haul [The Sun] 28, 31, 54, 55
- Traethodydd [The Essayist] 14

Welsh towns
  Aberystwyth xxxiv, 20, 114, 115, 189
  Bangor xviii, xxxvii, 1, 31, 47, 48, 57, 68, 101, 109, 114, 116, 120, 122, 129, 139, 148, 150, 151, 153, 158, 159, 162, 175, 189
  Beaumaris 47
  Caernarfon 14, 64, 98, 173
  Cardiff 48, 189
  Cardigan 21
  Carmarthen 13, 28
  Colwyn Bay 102, 137
  Denbigh 32
  Dolgellau 21, 75
  Dowlais 35, 55
  Lampeter xiv
  Llandudno 102, 104, 131, 162
  Machynlleth xiii, 10, 12, 19, 20, 30, 34, 53, 57, 58, 59, 60, 74, 75, 79, 146
  Merthyr Tydfil 48, 68
  Newport (Gwent) 18
  Portmadog 133
  Pwllheli 150
  Rhos 102, 113, 150
  Rhyl 106
  Rhymney 68
  St. David's (technically, a city) 31
  Welshpool 31, 38, 42, 50, 51
Welsh villages
  Abercegir 26
  Abergele 19, 48
  Aberhosan 40, 62, 139
  Abermaw 70
  Amlwch 46
  Bethesda 113, 151, 176
  Blackwood 18
  Brynsiencyn 110
  Bwlan 60, 128, 173
  Celli Dywyll 41
  Croesor 160
  Crosswood (Trawsgoed) 51
  Cwmcarnedd 13, 39, 80
  Cywarch 59
  Darowen iii, 10, 11, 12, 24, 31, 34, 42, 54, 59, 74, 140

Deiniolen (also Llanbabo) 105, 106, 171
Dinas Mawddwy 60
Dinorwic 25, 171
Dolfach 62
Dolwyddelan 142
Dwyran 110
Dylasau 145
Dylife 40
Fronfelen (Vronvelen) 51
Goginan 189
Llanasa 19
Llanbedr 20, 95
Llanbrynmair xiii, 12, 13, 25, 32, 39, 62, 66, 74, 78, 146
Llandrygarn 46
Llanfaes 46, 47, 48
Llangadfan 29, 93
Llangefni 19, 45, 46, 47
Llanllechid 151
Melinbyrhedyn 12, 16, 24, 26, 29, 38
Nant-y-Glo 18
Newborough 26, 110
Pentir 120
Pontrobert 38
Pont-y-pl 68
Porthaethwy (Menai Strait) 156
Talsarn 19, 20
Talybont 70
Talywern 139, 146
Trawsfynydd 95
Tredegar 18, 68
Trefnewydd (Newtown) 12, 34, 38, 39, 40, 43, 49, 51, 52
Tregaron 32, 114, 115, 146, 147, 189
Ysbyty Ifan xv, 141, 142, 143, 145
Werth, Alexander 163, 177
Weygand, Maxime 119, 121, 122, 135, 172
Williams, Tom Nefyn 159
Williams, Zephaniah 74
Workhouse 21, 22, 42

About the Author

W. Ambrose Bebb
[adapted from the original publisher's first (Welsh) editions]

William Ambrose Bebb was born on 4 August 1894 in Blaendyffryn, Goginan, near Aberystwyth, although he was raised at Camer, Tregaron. He attended elementary and shire schools in Tregaron. In 1914, he entered university at Aberystwyth; and in 1918 he graduated with honors in Welsh and History. Bebb earned his M.A. degree in 1920. From 1921 until 1925, he lectured in Welsh at the Sorbonne in Paris, during which time he traveled widely in France, Brittany and the Continent and also wrote extensively for *Y Faner* [*The Banner*], *Geninen* [*The Leek*] and *Breiz Atao* [*Brittany Forever*]. In 1925, he returned permanently to North Wales, where he lectured in History and Welsh at Normal College, Bangor.

During his lifetime, W. Ambrose Bebb was revered in Wales as a writer, historian, teacher and statesman. He was also a co-founder of the Welsh Nationalist Party whose *Plaid Cymru* members today constitute an increasingly visible presence in the British Parliament at Westminster and in the National Assembly for Wales at Cardiff. On 27

April 1955, while paying a house call between lectures at the College, Bebb died suddenly and unexpectedly some three months short of his 61st birthday.

Bebb was a prolific writer throughout his career, and some of his additional books include: *Llydaw* [*Brittany*]; *Crwydro'r Cyfandir* [*Roaming the Continent*]; *Dydd-Lyfr Pythefnos* [*A Fortnight's Diary*]; *Yr Argyfwng* [*The Crisis*]; *Ein Hen, Hen Hanes* [*Our Ancient, Ancient History*]; *Llywodraeth y Cestyll* [*A Government of Castles*]; *Cyfnod y Tuduriaid* [*The Age of the Tudors*]; *Machlud y Mynachlogydd* [*The Disappearance of the Monasteries*]; and *Machlud yr Oesoedd Canol* [*Twilight of the Middle Ages*]. The last five of these works have been translated by Marc K. Stengel, and they are currently being prepared for publication.

About the Translator

Marc K. Stengel

Marc K. Stengel, a dual-citizen of the U.S.A. and Canada, is a writer and translator living in Nashville, Tennessee.